**Future of Business a

The Future of Business and Finance book series features professional works aimed at defining, describing and charting the future trends in these fields. The focus is mainly on strategic directions, technological advances, challenges and solutions which may affect the way we do business tomorrow, including the future of sustainability and governance practices. Mainly written by practitioners, consultants and academic thinkers, the books are intended to spark and inform further discussions and developments.

Dominik Maximini

Agile Leadership in Practice

Applying Management 3.0

Second Edition

Springer

Dominik Maximini
ValueRise Consulting
Hattenhofen, Baden-Württemberg, Germany

ISSN 2662-2467 ISSN 2662-2475 (electronic)
Future of Business and Finance
ISBN 978-3-031-15024-1 ISBN 978-3-031-15022-7 (eBook)
https://doi.org/10.1007/978-3-031-15022-7

Original English edition published by BoD - Books on Demand, Norderstedt, 2018
1st edition: © Dominik Maximini 2018

© The Editor(s) (if applicable) and The Author(s), under exclusive license to Springer Nature Switzerland AG 2022
This work is subject to copyright. All rights are solely and exclusively licensed by the Publisher, whether the whole or part of the material is concerned, specifically the rights of translation, reprinting, reuse of illustrations, recitation, broadcasting, reproduction on microfilms or in any other physical way, and transmission or information storage and retrieval, electronic adaptation, computer software, or by similar or dissimilar methodology now known or hereafter developed.
The use of general descriptive names, registered names, trademarks, service marks, etc. in this publication does not imply, even in the absence of a specific statement, that such names are exempt from the relevant protective laws and regulations and therefore free for general use.
The publisher, the authors, and the editors are safe to assume that the advice and information in this book are believed to be true and accurate at the date of publication. Neither the publisher nor the authors or the editors give a warranty, expressed or implied, with respect to the material contained herein or for any errors or omissions that may have been made. The publisher remains neutral with regard to jurisdictional claims in published maps and institutional affiliations.

This Springer imprint is published by the registered company Springer Nature Switzerland AG
The registered company address is: Gewerbestrasse 11, 6330 Cham, Switzerland

Foreword

I once invited my team to do a code review in the sun. The weather was beautiful; we had a habit of discussing source code each week; there was a nice patch of green grass just outside our office, and I was in a joyful mood. So why not?

I also organized lunch meetings where employees shared their vacation photos. I invited colleagues to cook dinners in my kitchen. (Food is a recurring theme in my work-life.) I convinced our office manager to put up a bell that we could ring to mark celebrations (with cake or cookies, of course). And I used my office chair as a wheelchair while visiting teams across the entire office, a practice that I consider naming Management By Rolling Around (MBRA). Some people thought I was a silly manager.

Several years later, when I quit my job as a development manager to become a writer and speaker, one team member told me that I was "the best manager he had ever worked with." Another person said I was "the first manager who didn't suck." Some experts say that, when employees quit, they usually do so because of their managers. But not in my case. I had evidence that, in my part of the organization, turnover dropped to nearly zero. Sure, I was probably a silly manager, but my team members stayed! And my CEO was pleased.

Whether I was indeed a good manager, or just the first one who didn't suck, it was clear that I managed things differently compared to others. I had no fear of experimenting with unconventional ideas. I wasn't interested in implementing management practices just because they were the norm in other organizations. I cared much more about practices that had a positive impact on people's happiness, engagement, and productivity.

When I started writing about my alternative approach to management, which I named "Management 3.0," some managers in other organizations started copying my practices with their own teams. A few of them even wanted to know all the details, variations, and exceptions for each practice. I received questions similar to "How long does it take to do a code review in the sun?" "Is it OK for the team to sit in the shade?" and "What do you do when it's raining?"

As a writer and speaker, I share management practices that worked for me (and some practices used by other managers and their teams). What worked for me could work for you. But there are no guarantees. And I cannot share all the details, variations, and exceptions, because I don't know them. You will have to try for yourself and see if you can replicate the successes. Every good practice for me is an experiment for you! That was always the best advice I could give to anyone who asked for more.

Until now.

It was with great pleasure that I learned about this new book written by Dominik Maximini. Dominik has been experimenting with nearly all Management 3.0 practices as described in my works. With many of them, Dominik succeeded. With some, he failed. But when Dominik failed, he figured out how to change the practices and make them work in his situation. And with other ideas, he was able to venture far beyond what I had experienced or even imagined myself.

Managers are like chefs. (I warned you about my food obsession.) Chefs use standard recipes from books, but they always change things depending on their guests and the environment in which they need to cook. Great dishes should first be credited to the chefs who prepared them, and only second to the original recipes that they used while cooking.

In this book, Dominik shares all he knows about experimenting with Management 3.0 practices. Managers (and chefs) are best advised to improve their work, not just by reading more recipe books, but also by learning how other managers have experimented with and improved upon those recipes.

I am convinced that this book will help you be a better manager.

Rotterdam, Netherlands   Jurgen Appelo

Foreword

In October of 2008, I started at NovaTec as Business Unit Manager (back then a totally undefined role) for the specialist area of software architecture. Up to that point in my professional career, I had worked as software developer, software architect, and IT consultant, 10 years of which with IBM. My expertise and experience in management was unfortunately limited. After successively taking on management activities and ultimately becoming a NovaTec board member in 2015, it was very valuable for me to have colleagues like Dominik Maximini in the company, who focused full-time on company cultures and management practices as their specialist consulting area. Over the years, a synergy has developed between the idea generation in Dominik's specialist field and the experimentation with these new approaches within NovaTec itself. As a decision maker, it was my responsibility to understand these good ideas and implement them together with the management team.

This book before you now describes the long change journey we have taken together with Dominik. I have learned a lot and am very pleased to have taken part on this journey. This journey, however, is far from over; we regularly encounter new potential for improvement and creativity. Among other things, we want to increase transparency within the company and allow our employees more space for forming something new. One of the next steps is to improve the working environment within NovaTec under the catch word "agile workplace." As part of this, we want to enable and support the best possible creative and collaborative working conditions. I am certain that during our implementation process we will continue to encounter new ideas for improvement that will serve our company even better still.

Our path to this point was not always easy, but looking back on the journey, it was a good decision to make the effort to implement the Management 3.0 principles. Today, we can already see that the changes have had a significant positive effect. In the meantime, we have established diverse metrics, that we now regularly monitor, and which have continuously improved over several years. One might assume that the agile values and Management 3.0 practices, e.g. employee satisfaction, only show benefit internally. It is however clearly obvious to us now that these changes also show a positive influence on traditional external business metrics like customer satisfaction and profitability.

One point that should always be kept in mind is the speed of change in connection with potential fatigue created by changing too quickly. Here you need to constantly find an optimum between the rate of change and the increased demands on those involved. I would be really pleased if other leaders could learn from our successes and our failures, and integrate these findings in their own future decisions and actions.

With this, I wish you success on your own agile journey!

NovaTec Consulting GmbH Konrad Pfeilsticker
Stuttgart, Germany

Foreword

A New View on Management

Our economies are changing rapidly. Product life cycles are getting shorter, market and customer demands are constantly changing. Customers are no longer looking for a product but rather for a specific solution which best fits their own specific needs. New technologies arise and offer radically new approaches for solving existing problems as well as offering new options. Old competencies are losing relevance, new competencies are in demand. When working with students, committees, and leaders these topics are dominant and lead me to the insight that these changes are significantly impacting the work of today's managers.

This creates conflict between employees and managers, especially when considering established management structures and styles. Employees no longer want to be "traditionally" led, as the demands upon them are soaring. They demand the right to have a say in more matters and expect their own needs to receive a central focus.

Adapting the organization to increasingly important external influences, namely organizational change, also requires the active role of management. Without active leadership, successful change will not happen.

Dominik's new book is based on many years of experience in management consulting, and with applying new management techniques in agile environments. He is focusing on successful change management especially highlighting the principles of building teams, as well as the necessary changes in organizational structure, leadership, and focus of the organization. These changes also have to be supported by other systems, for example those used for performance measurement or reward distribution. His book is an integrated, holistic approach covering all the relevant aspects necessary to achieve successful modern-day change management. He excellently describes how the role of leaders needs to evolve in our rapidly changing business world.

Dominik's approach is unique for that matter and transports an integrated agile management approach. This integrated approach is especially important in times of dramatic change and helps managers to shape a new vision for their role. All stakeholders are integrated and become partners in the change process, forming a robust foundation for future profitable growth.

University of Lucerne, Senator of the European
Economic Forum (EWIF—Europäisches
Wirtschaftsforum e.V.)
Lucerne, Switzerland

Claus W. Gerberich

What You Should Expect from This Book

This book is an experience report, based on 7 years of my work in a single company, originally written in 2017. Although I am a consultant, this book does not tell you anything about my customers. Even though our customers influenced many of our decisions, this book doesn't tell their story. It is purely focused on telling the story of NovaTec, a 200-person Germany-based IT consulting organization. While the descriptions of what we did are accurate, their interpretations represent my personal opinion, or the opinion of the people cited. You should not conclude that everything that worked for us will work for you. Your situation is unique; what you read here could help, on the other hand it could create chaos!

I strongly recommend running experiments. If something appeals to you, figure out how to run an experiment in a contained environment. If that succeeds, go ahead and try a larger one. At all times make sure you are engaging your primary agile tool: Namely, your brain.

Please do not expect this book to be a blueprint for your own journey toward Agility. Take it for what it is: A collection of stories, experienced by somebody else, that might inspire you, but were not designed for your own individual environment.

Acknowledgements

Thank you for reading this book. Without your interest in it, the effort would have been needlessly spent. Also, I want to thank the people who made this work possible. Foremost my family, who endured my absence while writing. Second, my team who never flinched when I started talking about this book—again and again. The NovaTec management board, who provided their full support and used the writing and review process as a catalyst for change. Glenn Lamming, who helped with a keen eye to soften the edges of my German style when writing in English. And of course the many other reviewers and contributors, namely:

- Jurgen Appelo
- Claus W. Gerberich
- Konrad Pfeilsticker
- Michael Schuchart
- Hans-Dieter Brenner
- Stefan Bleicher
- Juliane Pilster
- Sven Diefenthäler
- Lutz Malburg
- Boris Steiner
- Christian Richter
- Marco Dietrich
- Christine Schmitt
- Stefan Mieth
- Dirk Maucher and
- Lars Dülfer

Thank you all!
Also feel free to get in touch with me—you can connect with me on LinkedIn.

Contents

1	**Context Is Everything**	1
	1.1 Organizational Culture	1
	1.2 Management 3.0	2
	1.3 The Market	3
	1.4 The Playing Field	3
	1.5 My Own Role	4
	1.6 The Timeline	6
2	**Building Teams**	9
	2.1 Getting to Know Each Other	9
	2.2 Building Trust	13
	2.3 Radical Transparency	19
	2.4 Establishing Values	27
	2.5 Hiring and Firing	32
	2.6 Learnings	35
3	**Changing Organizational Structure**	37
	3.1 Changes Within One Area	37
	3.2 Bigger Changes	39
	3.3 Satellite Sites	44
	3.4 Virtual Working	46
	3.5 Learnings	50
4	**Changing Leadership**	53
	4.1 Leadership and Management Tasks	53
	4.2 Leadership Style	57
	4.3 People Filling Leadership Positions	60
	4.4 Learnings	61
5	**Changing Focus**	63
	5.1 Focus of the Organization	63
	5.2 Focus of Managers	65
	5.3 Happiness	67
	5.4 Learnings	68

6	**Changing Measurement Systems**		71
	6.1	Measuring Success	71
	6.2	Measuring Happiness	75
	6.3	Measuring Money	79
	6.4	Learnings	84
7	**Changing Reward Systems**		85
	7.1	What Are Rewards?	85
	7.2	Who Gets Rewarded How by Whom	86
	7.3	Salary Systems	92
	7.4	Learnings	93
8	**Changing Career Paths**		95
	8.1	Consulting Career	95
	8.2	Specialist Career	96
	8.3	Management Career	100
	8.4	Learnings	105
9	**Changing Processes**		107
	9.1	Who Gets to Decide What?	107
	9.2	SMILE	113
	9.3	Project Selection	116
	9.4	Holiday Leave	118
	9.5	Hiring New Employees	119
	9.6	Career Coaching	121
	9.7	Organizing Management Work	123
	9.8	Learnings	124

The Phases	125
Appendix	127
Abbreviations	129
Literature	131
Index	133

List of Figures

Fig. 1.1	Dominik's task distribution	5
Fig. 1.2	Three phases	6
Fig. 2.1	Personal Maps example	12
Fig. 2.2	Moving Motivator cards	17
Fig. 2.3	Feedback workshop chart	22
Fig. 2.4	Salary workshop chart	26
Fig. 2.5	Our competence area values	27
Fig. 2.6	Our Kudo Wall	30
Fig. 2.7	Example Kudo Card	31
Fig. 2.8	Bonusly example rewards	32
Fig. 3.1	Phase one competence area structure	38
Fig. 3.2	Original organizational structure	40
Fig. 3.3	Competence area manager duties	41
Fig. 3.4	Value creation units with a dominant central authority	42
Fig. 3.5	The virtual distance model (cf. Sobel & Reilly, 2008, p. 48)	46
Fig. 4.1	Complexity domains, Based on Stacey (1996, p. 47) and Schwaber and Beedle (2002, p. 93)	58
Fig. 5.1	Phase one focus	64
Fig. 5.2	2017 focus	65
Fig. 6.1	Net promoter score distribution	75
Fig. 6.2	Net promoter score evolution at NovaTec	76
Fig. 6.3	Agile methods sales and earnings	80
Fig. 6.4	Results per employee compared to 2010	81
Fig. 6.5	Average customer productive days per week	82
Fig. 6.6	Employee turnover (percentage of staff)	82
Fig. 8.1	Career models are changing	96
Fig. 9.1	Delegation Board	108
Fig. 9.2	SMILE idea entry form	114
Fig. 9.3	2017 agile job advertisement	120

List of Tables

Table 6.1	Overall results	77
Table 6.2	Results grouped by general domain	77
Table 6.3	Overall results grouped by tenure	77
Table 6.4	Overall results grouped by career level	77
Table 6.5	Criticism from the open text field	78
Table 7.1	Rewards mapped to intrinsic Management 3.0 motivators	91
Table 8.1	NovaTec career levels	96
Table 8.2	Promotion criteria at NovaTec (consulting career)	97
Table 8.3	Differences between the specialist and the consulting career	101
Table 8.4	Competency framework for Scrum Masters	102
Table 9.1	Seven levels of delegation	108
Table 9.2	Delegation levels viewed from the source of power	108
Table 9.3	Delegation levels defined	109
Table 9.4	Deciding on delegation levels	110
Table 9.5	Topics to decide about	110
Table 9.6	Delegation Board version one	111
Table 9.7	Today's Delegation Board	112
Table 9.8	SMILE vote minimums	115
Table 9.9	SMILE ideas and costs	116
Table 9.10	SMILE ideas implemented by management	117

Context Is Everything   1

Before we dive into the details of our agile journey, you should understand our context. Only when you understand the circumstances, will you have a fair chance of judging the use of what you read for your own situation.

1.1 Organizational Culture

Introducing agile methods into an enterprise almost always causes the existing organizational culture to change. If you want to understand the details of culture, you can find a multitude of authors who talk about it. For example, you can read my book "The Scrum Culture" (Maximini, 2015), upon which this chapter is based.

Personally, I prefer Schneider's brief definition: "Organizational culture is the way we do things in order to succeed" (1999, p. 128). Ed Schein goes into more detail and specified three levels at which culture manifests (cf. Schein, 2009, pp. 39–40):

1. External Survival Issues.
2. Internal Integration Issues.
3. Deeper Underlying Assumptions.

The external survival issues are everything an external visitor can observe in the enterprise: Company mission and vision, strategy, goals, and the means to implement them. This involves organizational structure, the systems and processes being used, including error-detection and correction.

Internal integration issues cover the parts of a culture only an employee of the company can perceive after some time in the organization. External visitors most likely will not be able to identify these aspects. They include the usage of a common language and common concepts as well as the answer to the question who is an "insider" and who is an "outsider." Essentially, group boundaries and identity are defined on this level. The internal integration issues also describe how status and rewards are allocated, how authority is distributed, and how work relationships are established between people. For example, authority could be distributed based on technical knowledge (the one most knowledgeable on the issue at hand is followed) or based on position (the one with the most stripes on the shoulder has the last say).

The deeper underlying assumptions are difficult to name even for people who have been with the company for many years. They contain basic assumptions about what makes the world go round, including questions like:

- What is the relationship of humans to nature like?
- What is reality?
- How is truth defined?
- What comprises the human nature?
- What defines human relationships?
- What is the nature of time and space?
- What do we believe about the unknowable and uncontrollable?

These questions are rather more philosophic than economic. In a business context, you only encounter them on rare occasions. However, they do have a huge impact on our everyday actions. Imagine two people coming from different cultures: One person believes it to be absolutely true that time is absolute and static. Once gone, it's over and lost. The other person is absolutely sure that time is elastic, moving relatively compared to the situation. A sentence like: "The project must be finished by date X" will be interpreted significantly different by these two people...

I will not go deeper into the theory of organizational culture. This book is also not structured using the three levels Schein defined. Instead, you will find spotlights on specific things we tried and changed. With the knowledge about organizational culture in the back of your mind, you will be able to recognize the impact this had on our culture.

1.2 Management 3.0

Management 3.0 is a term coined by Jurgen Appelo in his book of the same title. It is a toolbox of agile management practices along with a set of principles that these practices must follow to qualify. All Management 3.0 practices are free to use and can be found at https://management30.com or in Jurgen's books, in particular in "Managing for Happiness." Whenever you read "Management 3.0" throughout this work, you know that we used one of these practices, and you know where to look it up for more information. You also know that the practice was taken from Jurgen's work.

You probably still wonder where the name comes from and what the number means. After all, we are talking about industry 4.0, so why do we still use Management 3.0? The answer is that Jurgen defined Management 1.0 as "Doing the wrong thing," which is basically tayloristic top-down management. In today's fast-paced world, you simply can no longer succeed with this type of management.

Management 2.0 is described as "doing the right thing wrong." This means, having great ideas like focusing on employees, teams, and quality, but using systemically flawed methods that do not look at the overall system to achieve that. Management 3.0 instead tries to look at organizations as complex adaptive systems and offers methods that are adequate for this kind of environment. Therefore, Jurgen defines it as "doing the right thing." If you prefer another name, that's fine. Personally, I prefer "agile leadership" as a general term. You will also notice throughout this book that we tried other methods that are not described by Management 3.0. That's fine. Management 3.0 is not a methodology that sends the process inquisition after you to throw you into purgatory. It's just a toolbox. Extend and adapt it, whenever you feel the need.

1.3 The Market

Economy is great right now. It's September 2017 and the unemployment rate in Germany hovers around 5.9% (Statista, 2017a). It has been declining steadily for years and new jobs have been created in many sectors, and in particular in IT. In southern Germany, where NovaTec is based, the unemployment rate is even lower at 3.6% (Statista, 2017b). That means we have more open job offers than people applying for them. This also leads to a very high demand for consultants, which is good for NovaTec. Also, the biggest industries in southern Germany, namely automotive and engineering are faced with the biggest challenges since they came in existence: Everything is digitized, even physical machines are starting to communicate with each other in the "Cloud." Cars, reconfigured to electrical engines, connected with all kinds of digital systems, will be driving autonomously in the near future and will be shared among multiple users (instead of being used by only a single person as today). This is all new and requires a huge amount of IT and process knowledge. To achieve this, almost all German companies are trying to "become agile" or "introduce agile methods." All this leads to an ever-increasing demand for agile consultancy. As a company focused on IT consulting, it is almost impossible to fail in this environment—as long as you have able employees to satisfy the demand. The challenge during the last years was to get and keep skilled employees who are happy in the company. Starting a business unit for agile consulting seems like a natural fit here.

1.4 The Playing Field

In September 2017, NovaTec is a 207 employees strong Germany-based IT consulting company, conducting business mainly in southern Germany and generating a revenue of roughly 24 million Euros per year. We have several branch offices, the most important ones being located in Frankfurt, Munich, and Granada. The goal is to deploy people near their home location, but it is normal for us to travel if the customer has a need for it. NovaTec is organized in "competence areas" (CAs).

These competence areas are fully accountable for their revenue, contribution margins, hiring and firing since 2017. They are basically autonomous business units. We are divided into the units of agile methods, agile quality engineering, application performance management, business process management, enterprise application development, enterprise architecture management, and IT architecture. So this structure is based on technical competence rather than industry or other focus.

We are earning money with three types of services: professional consulting, developing software for our customers, and training. The structure is primarily supporting the consultancy and training services. This is neither good nor bad, I just want to give you an idea of what to picture. Our employees usually work for our customers—either in our offices or at their sites—80–90% of their time (e.g., Monday to Thursday). The rest of their time is used for learning and building up work relationships. All competence areas consist of dispersed teams, so not everybody is living near the same branch office. Since all CAs are autonomous, each one deals differently with this situation. Each competence area is led by a "competence area manager" (CAM) whose primary qualification is technical excellence in his domain. These CAMs are reporting directly to the management board. In fact, they are all reporting to the same manager. To support all this, there are central functions like central services, billing, IT administration, human resources, sales, and marketing. These are reporting to different managers of the board. All CAs can use their services, in many cases this is even mandatory.

1.5 My Own Role

When I originally wrote this book in 2017, my role had multiple facets. About 3 days a week, I was working as a consultant, helping customers to implement agile methods or providing training to them. The rest of the time, I was working on tasks as the competence area manager for "agile methods." This means, on the one hand, people management and, on the other hand, working on team tasks as part of the team. In addition, I was the primary change agent inside NovaTec, meaning I was expected to suggest changes, conduct experiments, and work with the management board to implement good experiences on a larger scale (cf. Fig. 1.1).

If you want to understand the context, especially about my own person, it is not enough to know what I did back then. It is also important to understand where I came from professionally.

After studying Business Information Technologies in Trier, I worked for almost 4 years with Carl Zeiss. We founded a startup, by taking it out of the corporate Research Division. The goal was to create a product out of an idea and get it ready for serial production. Technically we were successful—but not so on the business side. In 2009 we even won an innovation award for "innovative business design." This was the place where I first came into contact with agile methods. One sunny day my boss walked up to me and said: "Dominik, you will be our Scrum Master from today on." While that certainly sounded like a cool title, I didn't have a clue what

1.5 My Own Role

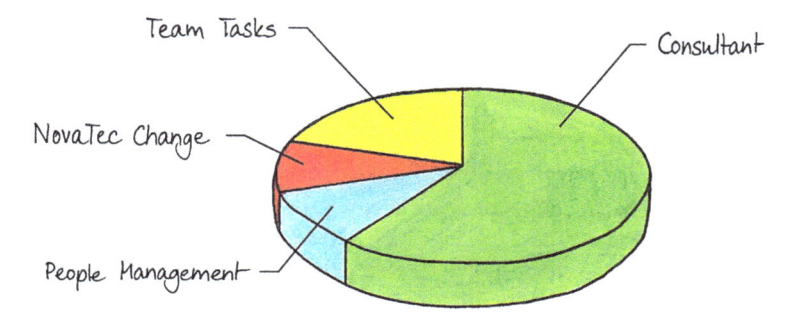

Fig. 1.1 Dominik's task distribution

"Scrum" was. So I asked for a training but was given a book instead, followed by the advice that trainings were expensive and I was certainly smart enough to figure it out all by myself. So I was now able to practice with three teams: One doing regular software development, one doing research, and one doing hardware development. Of course we all tried our best, but without proper support or education we often stumbled and probably made every single mistake possible. During that time, I realized my interest for leadership and management. Compared to my boss I had fundamentally different views on many questions, especially business ones. We discussed them with great enthusiasm. I liked that, it taught me fact-based discussion and I am still trying to use this technique every day. We also had completely diverging management styles. I tried to leave decisions to the teams and stick to them for a while while my boss tried to make the decisions himself and tended to change them several times a week. It was a great opportunity that I could observe and experience these different styles myself, including their consequences. After three and a half years the relationship between my boss and myself changed. The discussions became more heated and less fact-based. In the end we couldn't agree on the question if age per se had something to do with the quality of decisions, so I left. At that time I had learned so much that I had already qualified as a "Professional Scrum Trainer" with the recently founded Scrum.org. Helping and teaching others is a strong motivator for me, so I decided to become a consultant. My application at NovaTec was accepted and I had been working there for more than 7 years in 2017 when I wrote this book. The environment allowed me to thrive, to further deepen my knowledge and experience. I worked my way deeply into Scrum, organizational change, and agile leadership. The feedback from customers and colleagues added additional motivation, allowing me to write two books and doing a part-time MBA in the evenings. Helping build a local agile community, supporting the Scrum.org trainer network and speaking on some conferences supplies me with a never-ending flow of new impressions and additional learning opportunities. These facts also created a level of trust with NovaTec's management board that led them to ask me to build up the competence area of agile methods. This was a great opportunity since I could finally apply all the knowledge and experience from my customers' teams to my own team. To support this, I studied Management 3.0 and became a facilitator.

We lived this leadership style every day and were truly successful with it. Two years later, I left NovaTec and founded my own company, ValueRise Consulting.

1.6 The Timeline

When we look at the last couple of years at NovaTec, there are three phases that are important for you to understand (cf. Fig. 1.2). All the experiments conducted and the decisions made fall into one or more of these phases and were influenced by them.

The first phase was relevant in my first years at NovaTec. I was a regular consultant. In my job interview, the COO told me that he wasn't sure if he should hire me since I was not very experienced in JAVA development. Well, that wasn't the job I had applied for... During that phase, I spent almost 40 h a week with customers. My title was "consultant," later "senior consultant," and my impact at NovaTec was restricted to the team I was part of. Even there it was small. We were three people: One competence area manager, one Competence Group Manager (comparable to a team lead) and myself, the worker.

The second phase was mainly influenced by a struggle inside the management board. During that time, there were three members of the board. One of them (the CEO) was finally ousted by the others, and two other managers (the CTO and the COO) were promoted into the board. In 2017, referenced as "today" throughout this book, there were still these four members in the management board. This period of time was very volatile. On the one hand, everything was paralyzed for almost 2 years, no strategic decisions were made by the board. On the other hand, this experience created an urgency for change and opened ears for suggestions. In addition, our board members were content in high-level strategic alignment, so we were pretty much unconstrained in what we were doing inside the business units. This helped us to conduct more risky experiments and go a little bit beyond our competence area borders.

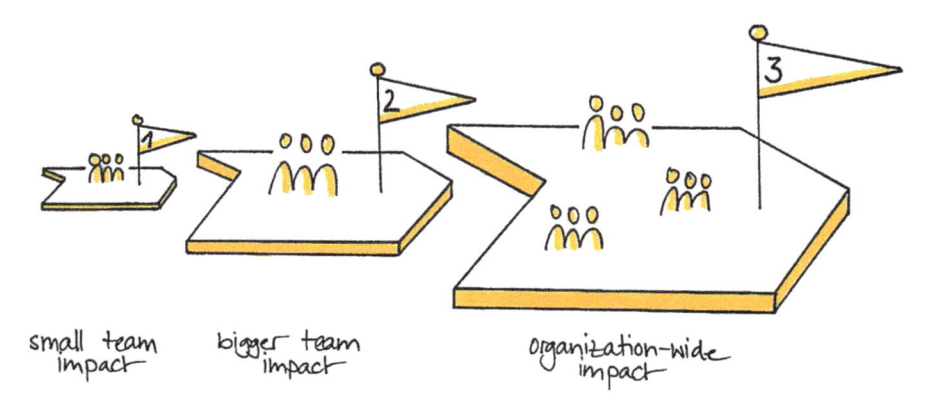

Fig. 1.2 Three phases

1.6 The Timeline

The third phase is still ongoing. The difficult process of parting with the CEO is now completed, and the whole board is full of energy working to create a thriving company. Even though some employees left together with the old CEO, this was healthy for the overall organization, allowing us to create a more homogenous culture—and again increasing the readiness for change. In this phase, we are trying experiments on a large scale, affecting the whole company. This is where the big wheels are turned.

It is important to keep track of these phases when reading this book. I constantly refer to them so you can easily understand why we acted a certain way in a specific situation. Without context, it is hard to judge if something could also work in your organization. At the end of this book in Chap. 11 you will find a short description of these phases—you might want to refer to this for further clarity.

Building Teams

2

You now have an idea of our general situation and setup. The remainder of the book describes the experiments we tried and the results they yielded. Since building a team is always a good place to start with (and agile leadership relies on self-organizing teams), I will dive into this topic first. Please be aware that building a team is never over. While the effort you as the leader invest is higher in the beginning, it will never drop to zero. Even if no one leaves or joins the team, individual people develop and change all the time, causing the complex adaptive system called "team" to change as well. On top of that, all aspects of leadership are related to each other. For example, team- and trust-building are closely related to one another, as well as to basically all other areas of change in this book.

2.1 Getting to Know Each Other

Self-organizing teams are something special. They don't come into existence just by being announced, nor do they suddenly appear on stage after Scrum or another agile method was introduced. Many people aren't used to self-organization. Even my team, after several years of practicing agile leadership and teaching agile thinking to others, isn't fully self-organizing (I believe them to be at around 95%). However, before we can start thinking about self-organization, we must think about becoming a team. Teams are definitely not the same as workgroups. Teams are more than the sum of the individual performances of their members. Teams work toward the same goals. Team members care for each other. A team is not created by putting names into a spreadsheet and hoping for the best. It actually is hard work to get there. The ultimate ingredient for becoming a team is trust. The prerequisite of trust is really getting to know each other, because the average human being only cares for people she really knows. Think about it for a moment: What generates more emotions in yourself—when a person is killed in a remote country or when your neighbor has his lawnmower stolen out of his garage? Ethically, it should be the person who was killed. In reality, it is probably your neighbor. I am not a social scientist, so I cannot explain this phenomenon properly. When you are trying to become part of a team however, you should know about it and use it. The first step you have to achieve is to get people to care for one another. In addition, I purposefully wrote "become part of a team." You can't just "make them" become a team. You are either part of it, or you will fail.

The first thing we tried to get to know each other was working in workshops. We could fully focus on the factual level, working together on real-life problems. This worked well on many occasions, but failed miserably on others. After some time, we realized that we could not keep the relationship level out of the game. Workshop results were too low in quality and quantity. We discussed simple matters for ages to no avail. Working in workshops wasn't enough. It was necessary though: The general format of a workshop allowed us to involve everybody, ignoring hierarchies and focusing on one question at a time. We learned about each other and observed ourselves at work. Even though it wasn't enough, we were building the foundation for further action.

When we had learned to include the relationship level, we started to talk more about private matters. How was family doing? What were the hobbies of our colleagues? In phase one, we didn't formalize this but rather threw in private comments every now and then and showed interest for each other. For example, I listened to a set of black and death metal CDs one of our team members liked, to show respect for him and verify my dislike of this type of music (unfortunately, it didn't change). With the same team member, I shared experiences of video games, because we both liked the same type of games. This brought us one tiny step closer together. We were three people at the time, and one of us refused to share anything private. We didn't know about his hobbies, we hardly knew anything about his family and we didn't know anything about his emotional world. We respected his stance, but that kept us locked into a non-team-state. We failed back then. From phase two on, we remedied this by demanding at least a basic amount of sharing from everybody and by providing a setting where everybody feels comfortable to share at least something. It is perfectly okay if you don't want to share everything, but it is not okay for you to not share anything. Back then, the person who refused to share anything became unhappy with us when we started sharing without his involvement, and he subsequently left the group. Today, if people don't share, we don't hire them.

This taught us a valuable lesson about everybody, including you and me: We have to share some things about ourselves. I am a very fact-based person, only sharing emotions with very few people in my life. For my team, I changed. I learned to read and speak my emotions and I started to share much more private information than I believed I would feel comfortable with. But I did and still do, because if everybody shares, a high level of relatedness is generated and treated with respect and confidentiality. Don't get me wrong, I won't be marrying my team and there are certainly things I still want to keep to myself. However I can only expect my team to develop trust when I act trustingly myself, and this starts with building a personal relationship.

2.1 Getting to Know Each Other

Recently, I saw a recruiting video from a large company. It showed employees performing their hobbies in a manufacturing plant. You could see the products of this company in the background. The message of this video was "hey, look at what cool people we have working here." Unfortunately, all the people stated on screen was that they were using their true skills in their private time—nobody mentioned using them during work. For me, practicing agile leadership, this was completely absurd. These people could only be themselves after work, could only use their great skills when they left the company premises. My belief is that everybody should be allowed to be him- or herself, also at work. You can only use these skills, if the team knows about them. So everything starts with sharing.

The first time we started to formalize sharing was during phase two as we got together on the sidelines at our annual Christmas party. The team composition had changed and most people didn't know each other well. I grabbed everybody with their drinks and we stood at a table. The music was still audible but not too loud, and the place we had chosen wasn't too busy, so we had a kind of private space for ourselves. I shared with everybody how interested I was in getting to know them better and wanted to learn more about them. To start it off I shared some stuff about myself. At that time, it was mostly stuff you could find when Googling me, but for the team this was new. They liked the idea and shared some aspects of their lives as well. Everybody to the extent he felt comfortable with at that moment. It was amazing what amount of experience, skills, and traits we had assembled at that table! None of us knew this before and our respect for each other rose rapidly that evening. Even months later, people were referring to that talk and expressed their appreciation. For me, this was a highly successful experiment.

Later, we learned about the Management 3.0 practice of "Personal Maps" (cf. Fig. 2.1). This practice is really simple. Everybody writes their name into the middle of a paper chart, a whiteboard, or other media, and creates a mind map from there. Each branch describes a category, which is self-defined by the person drawing the map. It could be family, business, hobbies, pets, traveling, or anything else the person believes to be important enough to share. Then, when everybody created their maps, they are presented, usually by somebody who did not draw that particular map themselves.

We quickly tried it out and loved it.

Everybody participated and we learned something new about every single-team member. In fact, we liked it so much that we hung the maps up in our team room so everybody could see them. Even though nobody had to, everybody put theirs up on the wall. Using Personal Maps is the most structured, effective, and fun way I know to share information about yourself and getting to know each other. I strongly recommend it.

Unfortunately, when we grew in size, the wall we used to show our maps was eliminated and some of the pictures were lost. Also, some of today's team members were not yet represented. Luckily, the team suggested to repeat this exercise again soon, and I am very happy to participate. It is no longer me who has to encourage sharing, it is the team who does this by themselves.

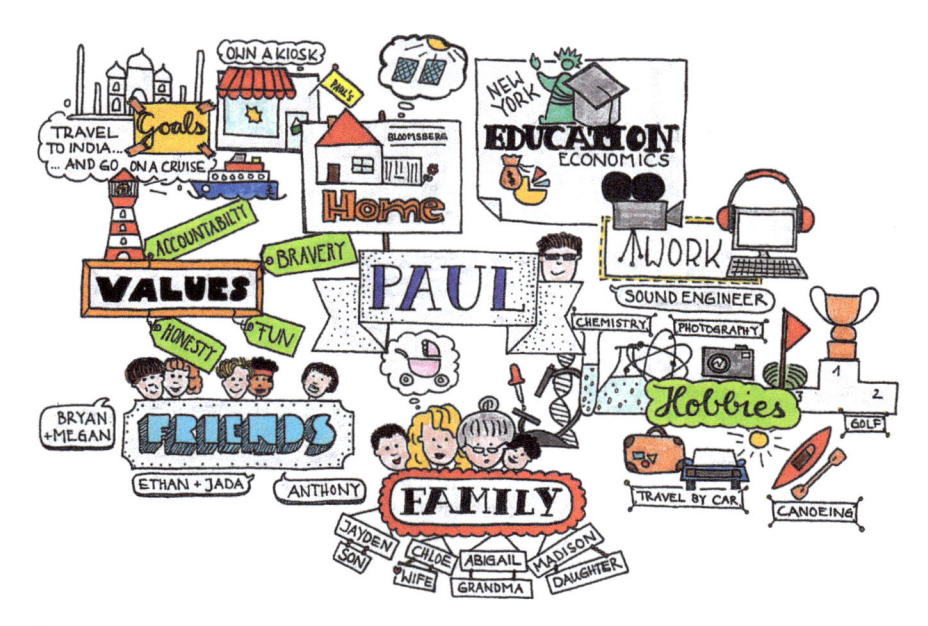

Fig. 2.1 Personal Maps example

One cool way the team came up with, to get to know each other better, is the institution of a "CFO." This Chief Fun Officer has the job to organize the next-next team event, so we always know what the next event will be and who will take care of the one after that. If you are the CFO, it is part of your duties to find the next CFO. So far, we didn't face any issues there, we always had enough volunteers. At least every quarter, often more frequently, we hold a team event.

While we do have a budget for this type of activity, we hardly ever use it. Some examples of activities include a team escape challenge, 3D outdoor archery parcours, having a barbecue together, and many more. In every single case, we learned something about us as a team and about the individual who had organized the event. We mastered the escape challenge so quickly that the owner of the place was mad at us because he couldn't give us many hints—a great experience for us as a team. Playing Robin Hood in the forest showed us how one of our team members spends his recreational time, gains his balance and focus. It also showed us how the manager (me) can hit a tiny rubber imitation squirrel but not the giant Grizzly bear—that created a good laugh and proved that making mistakes is okay for everybody. The CFO for the barbecue event was me. I wanted to show everybody what was most important for me at the time: My family and rebuilding our house. We practically barbecued at a construction site and learned that we could relax even in such an environment.

The CFO idea was and still is great. The only problem we faced so far is the name. Our "real" CFO was quite puzzled when he found out that we had multiplied his title. Luckily, he quickly got used to the idea.

All the experiments above were successful in that we learned about each other. However, they all require a certain amount of trust. As you can see in the chronology, we started with experiments that require a very low amount of trust and gained a little success by it. We continued with more trust-demanding activities and had greater successes. Today, it's a self-propelled system: Every activity requires and generates trust at the same time.

2.2 Building Trust

As you have seen in the chapter above, getting to know each other is not only a prerequisite for trust, but it is also trust-generating. However, you can do much more to increase the level of trust in your team. The simplest, but not easiest, component of your action must be to walk the talk. Whether you are asking for transparency, propagating a no-blame culture, or want to show appreciation for others, you have to be a role model in all of these questions. For example, in my first year at NovaTec I made a couple of suggestions for process improvements to my superior. He thanked me for it and I didn't hear back for half a year. Then, in the yearly performance appraisal meeting, he threw my suggestions back into my face, declaring that I was "not loyal" to the company if I came up with improvements. This damaged our relationship and made a trustful environment impossible, so I was assigned to another boss and I didn't shed any tears when my previous manager left the company some time later. Such stupid remarks can cause the team to not function at all for quite some time. Damage done that could have been prevented, if my superior had walked the right talk.

Now, allowing mistakes is very important in a complex environment, because you can only find solutions to novel problems if you allow experimentation. On top of this, only experiments that can fail are worth trying at all in the first place. In the example above, describing the situation in the yearly performance appraisal meeting, that means he repeated the same mistake several times. That is important to remember: In agile leadership, people are expected to make mistakes. However, they are not expected to repeat the same mistakes over and over again. Mistakes are intended to further learning—if no learning happens, then there is no use in making mistakes. An agile manager should therefore support learning and help to minimize repeated failure. A minimum requirement in this regard is for the leader to also actively show her own mistakes as well. If the boss says that she allows mistakes but never fails herself, then credibility is compromised. For example, I recently messed up. Every now and then, I have a conflict with one specific team mate. Mostly misunderstandings, nothing serious. Some time ago we agreed to immediately call each other when we disapprove of something the other person did, to not allow small issues grow into big ones. A couple of weeks ago, something happened that drove up my pulse. I should have called my colleague, but I didn't. Instead, I sent an email that in turn took him off balance. I had some zillion reasons to do so, but the bottom line is that it was very bad behavior from my side. So I walked up to him the next day and apologized. I as the manager admitted my mistake and showed that I am fallible.

This example also shows us the second pillar in building trust: Don't send emails for serious topics. Email (as well as all other asynchronous non-verbal communications) is a great tool to distribute information, but an awful one for discussion or conflict resolution. Especially if the level of trust within the team is low, emails will be interpreted in a way that doesn't solve problems but creates new ones. As an agile leader, you should consider email an invention of the devil, designed to corrupt your team. Instead, walk up to your team colleague and talk to him eye-to-eye. If you cannot do that, set up a video call. Again, eye-to-eye contact is what you want to achieve. If that means you have to sleep the issue over, even better. Sometimes that already solves it. In case a video call is not possible, then make a voice call. Listening to live spoken words is better than reading dead ones on a screen. It's bidirectional rather than unidirectional communication. If you want to send a summary of your talk via email to the other person once you are done—fine. Just try to avoid doing it as the first step. Showing that you go the extra mile for your team mates, not choosing the easy way, raises trust.

In a personal conversation scenario, a lot of information is conveyed without saying a single word. You can see if your colleague is tired, sick, or in a good mood. You can decide in the blink of an eye if it is a good moment for you to address the issue at hand. If there is a misunderstanding, he can ask back and you can clarify it right away. The required translation effort from your colleague is far less than if he has to read a written text. If you don't find any way around it and just have to send an email for a critical issue like criticism, make sure at least that the other person understands your context. A nice way to do it is described as "Feedback Wraps" in Management 3.0. They follow five steps (cf. Management3.0a):

1. Describe your context
2. List your observations
3. Express your emotions
4. Sort by value
5. End with suggestions

Imagine your colleague (let's call him Joe) did not deliver a slide for a workshop at a customer's site to the date agreed upon. You need that slide, because the customer is expecting it and you don't have the information required to build it yourself. You try to call your colleague, but don't get through. The following (without the headlines and numbering) might be the email you send to him:
1. Describe your context

Hi Joe,
It is the last day before the workshop at the customer and I am just making sure I am fully prepared for it. Today was packed with work and I am a little bit stressed out.

2. List your observations

While looking through my email, I could not find the slide you wanted to send to me. This slide is still important for the customer and therefore for me as well.
3. Express your emotions

This makes me nervous and anxious because I do want to do a good job tomorrow and feel that I can't without this slide.
4. Sort by value

The highest value for me is the information you wanted to put into the slide. The slide itself would be nice as well, but the information is more important to me. Either way, I need it by eight o'clock tomorrow morning.
5. End with suggestions

Please let me know how I can help you. For example, I can create the slide as such myself and you just deliver the information. If there is anything else you need, just give me a call.

When I learned about this practice for the first time, I was surprised by the meaning behind some of the steps. Let's quickly walk through them again. Describing your context is straightforward. You try to allow the other person to understand your state of mind at the time of writing the email. Interestingly, sometimes it is wise to include incidents outside work. Imagine you slept badly, your kid is sick or you had an argument with your wife in the morning—all this might influence the phrasing of your email even though your colleague is innocent and oblivious of these facts.

Then, list your observations. Emotions do not have a place here. Just write down the facts relevant for this specific situation. Personally, these first two steps help me getting my head clear. There have even been instances where I didn't continue writing the email because I realized I was only venting my own frustrations.

Then it's finally time for your emotions. Write down how you feel and what is causing you to feel like that. Help the other person understand your emotions. By clearly separating observations from emotions, you make it easier for your colleague to empathize with you.

The next step, sort by value, can easily be misunderstood. It is about explaining what actions of the other person would help you and thus provide value to you. Basically, you write down what you need. It is *not* about sorting all the points of criticism or your emotions. Don't get it wrong please—I did once and it caused great nausea.

Finally, make a request and offer your help. Show the other person that you are willing to support. This is not meant as a stick ("deliver now, or. . ."), it is meant to provide clarity, especially if the email already has become long. By offering your support, you open the door for further communication.

Our experience with Feedback Wraps is ambiguous. At first, we used them for in-person dialogues and they didn't work at all. It felt totally awkward and wasn't even useful as a training setup. Well, that's the sort of thing that happens if you try to hammer a screw into the wall. We then used them a couple of times for big issues, which didn't work either. The emails grew too big and the other person couldn't digest that amount of criticism. So, I strongly suggest you stick with in-person discussion for bigger problems. However, for smaller issues, as in the example above, Feedback Wraps work very well. We use them frequently, especially with people outside our team (we meet once a week, so we can solve most issues in person). For example, we had several issues with our inside sales officer. At first, we sent regular emails or tried feedback sandwiches (compliment—criticism—compliment) when we couldn't talk, but that didn't work and only widened the chasm. Then we moved to Feedback Wraps and got back into the conversation, finding ways to improve the situation. Today we live an equilibrium that works without frequent conflict and leverages the abilities of everybody involved.

"We" gives a hint toward another important practice to foster trust: solve issues as a team and share authority. Later in this book you will find the chapter "9.1 Who Gets to Decide What," which describes sharing authority in detail, albeit solving issues as a team is a general practice we should discuss here.

If you face an issue, involve the team. That does not necessarily mean that you or the manager does everything the team says. It means you open up to the team, show vulnerability since you obviously couldn't solve the issue alone and you trust the team to come up with good ideas. Actually, my personal experience shows that my team always gives me at least an additional perspective if not a better solution than my own. This is no surprise since ten brains should be smarter than a single one. Going through pain together, learning about problem-solving capabilities of each individual and seeing what everybody considers to be a problem brings the team closer together. We made this a habit in phase two when we defined team values, one of which still is "we never walk alone." So whenever anybody has any kind of issue, we try to solve it as a team. If the whole team isn't appropriate or available, a subset of the team helps. This can mean a late phone call, a Sunday morning breakfast, having lunch together, a little workshop on Friday or anything else you can imagine. Some of us consider this the glue that sticks us together. For example, when the issues with our inside sales officer began to fester, we first discussed them inside the team to make sure they were not an isolated observation by a single individual. Then, we brainstormed solutions and I discussed them (as the manager) with the sales officer. When this didn't improve the situation, we did a workshop with the person with the goal to include her in the team, as a full team member, to allow her to experience and share our level of trust and experience—or to find another solution. While she didn't want to join the team, we indeed found solutions to many issues and also understood her situation much better, which in turn reduced our expectation and demand from her. This reconstituted trust and led to a functioning agreement of how to work together, which is still in place.

Also, if you allow the team to make some types of decisions—and don't question them afterwards—you can increase their trust in you trusting them. This actually relieves you of some tasks and frees up time you can use better elsewhere.

2.2 Building Trust

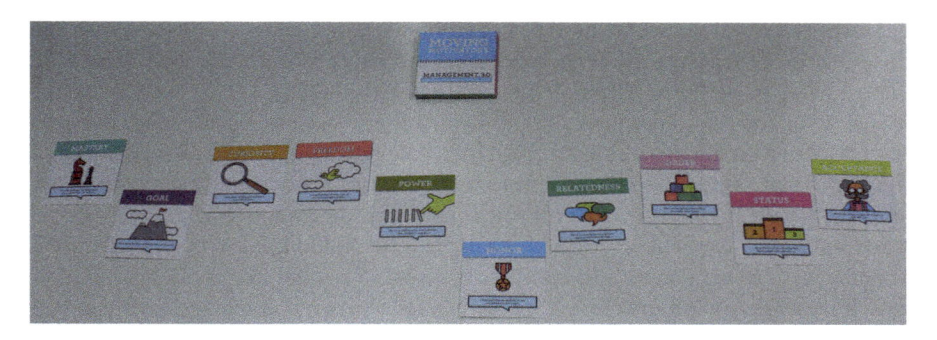

Fig. 2.2 Moving Motivator cards

There are hundreds of other ways to increase trust. I want to share two more with you. If you want to share authority, you need to know whom you are sharing it with. You also need to find out if that person or group wants to have authority shared. Basically, you have to understand where the other person is coming from. A Management 3.0 practice that is well suited to answer this question is "Moving Motivators" (cf. Management3.0b). It is quite simple: You get (or just print and cut) a set of ten cards (cf. Fig. 2.2). They resemble intrinsic desires. Money is not printed on them since money is an extrinsic motivator and we can expect most people to want to earn some money anyway. This practice just focuses on other desires your team mates are personally driven by. If a strong desire for somebody is missing, just create an additional card or rephrase an existing one. It's about your desires, not mine. The standard cards and explanations are:

- Acceptance—The people around me approve of what I do and who I am
- Curiosity—I have plenty of things to investigate and to think about
- Freedom—I am independent of others with my own work and responsibilities
- Status—My position is good, and recognized by the people who work with me
- Goal—My purpose in life is reflected in the work that I do
- Honor—I feel proud that my personal values are reflected in how I work
- Mastery—My work challenges my competence but it is still within my abilities
- Order—There are enough rules and policies for a stable environment
- Power—There's enough room for me to influence what happens around me
- Relatedness—I have good social contacts with the people in and around my work

You can try Moving Motivators both in an individual one-on-one environment and in a team setup. In our case, we were lucky because when I was accepted as a Management 3.0 facilitator, I used my team as the first test group to experiment a bit. When we reached the Moving Motivators exercise, we liked it and did it as a team. Later, we used it in some development dialogues. This is how it works (I'll use the group example here, the individual one works exactly the same):

You first explain every single card to the participants. This will lead to discussion since some people have a different understanding of certain cards. For example, in

Germany we always discuss "honor" at length, due to our history with this word and dictatorship. Discussing or even redefining the cards is perfectly fine. The only person who must know exactly what the card means for her is the one using it. Ask the people to order the cards: The most important one on one side, the least important one on the other side (cf. Fig. 2.2). If somebody wants to take cards out of the game, that's fine. Then ask people to form pairs (or do it publicly for everybody) and share their highlights. Also ask them to define their most and least important cards since your counterpart might use a different definition. Have them define their scale as well. Some people still consider the least important item somewhat important (it increases their motivation if it is there), for others it is actually demotivating if it is there. Do not constrain the numbers: Some people prefer to talk about just one or two cards, others want to explain all of them. Both are fine, we are trying to learn more about each other and build trust.

When you reached this point, you already learned a lot about your team. You will most certainly participate as well, so your team also learned a lot about you. When you do this exercise for the first time, you will notice that it makes you think about yourself. Sometimes you will want to repeat the exercise and some cards will end up in different places. However, the tendencies will usually remain the same. It may not really be all that important for the team to know, for example, that "Mastery" is number one or two for you. Yet, if this is crucial for you, the team should hear about it, which again increases trust. Therefore, you should conduct the exercise more than once.

The second part of Moving Motivators is to use it to get an idea of how changes affect the degree of fulfillment of your motivators. This is especially helpful in a development dialogue. Both of you lay the cards, as described above. Then, choose a biggish change for one of you. Often, this is a role change, a promotion, or a different customer. Imagine the situation after the change. Ask the question how this affects every single motivator. If the degree of fulfillment increases, move the card up—the higher the card, the higher the degree of fulfillment. If the degree of fulfillment decreases, move the card down. Of course, you only touch your own cards, so if you are discussing a promotion with your employee, he is the only one touching his cards. In some cases, you can add a couple of coaching questions to the mix. One could be: "How will the expectation of your boss change once you are promoted? How will this affect your motivators?"

This approach helps both of you to better understand what you really want, and to choose the right paths to get there.

We used Moving Motivators a couple of times in development dialogues but mainly stopped again, even though it was quite successful. The reason is that we found better ways to conduct this type of talk. However, I got the feeling that they would be helpful in our current situation and my intention is to start using them again to refresh our knowledge in the team about each other's motivators.

The last practice to increase trust I want to share with you is transparency. Say what you do and do what you say is the absolute minimum transparency you should provide. Transparency in fact can work both ways: It not only can increase trust, but it can also destroy it. Therefore, it is important enough to get its own chapter.

2.3 Radical Transparency

If you want to build teams, you are dependent on trust. If you want to build self-organizing teams, you are in additional need of transparency. A hundred years ago, people were not believed to be educated or smart enough to deal with all the necessary sorts of information for their work (Taylorism). Therefore, the less-smart workers were given more-smart managers to deal with the information for them and to tell them what to do. Today, people are generally well-educated and believed to be smart enough to work out what to do by themselves. Some advocate this applies only to innovation or knowledge work, but guess what: today almost every worker is a knowledge worker, no matter if he is sitting in an air-conditioned corner office or standing at a conveyor belt. The precondition for self-organization is transparency, because one can only make good decisions if the information required for it is ready at hand.

2.3.1 Sharing Information

When I started to work for NovaTec, there was a strict "no sharing" policy. Whatever information was available; it was kept to a few people trusted to "deal properly" with it. For example, at my first customer engagement as a consultant, I wasn't told what the negotiated daily rate for my work was. Asking my boss didn't help, because he didn't know either. I ended up talking to a member of the management board and was told that I couldn't know the information because I might use it for my next salary negotiations. Not knowing the information prevented me from negotiating higher daily rates with the customer and also kept me from figuring out what to do next in order to justify higher rates. I didn't like this situation, so I asked the customer to share the rates with me, which he did. Half a year later, I was able to negotiate significantly higher rates with the customer and presented the result to the board member, although at the time this did not lead to a different sharing policy. However, it was the door opener to being invited into the small group of people who were trusted to deal properly with information. Even before I accepted the role of competence area manager, I started to deal differently with transparency due to this experience. I started to strive for radical transparency.

In our competence area, we took the first step to transparency by discussing problems openly within the team. No matter who had what kind of issue, it was always an option (not an obligation) to discuss it within the team. The stronger our trust relationship grew; the more issues were discussed in the team. Today, I believe only very few issues are not taken to the team. The way this typically works is that somebody has some sort of problem (e.g., conflicts with somebody, challenging project situations or insecurities on how to proceed in personal development) and announces it in our weekly Scrum (we don't do dailies since we typically work with our customers from Monday to Thursday). Then we sit, stand, or squat together and discuss the issue. Usually we use a mixture of asking solution-oriented questions and offering tangible advice, depending on the situation. If the issue is between some of our team mates, we switch to a mediation mode and help the brawlers to see each other's positions. If the group workshop doesn't solve the issue, the colleagues involved choose their coaches from the team and continue to work on the issue individually until they feel the need to work on it together again. This procedure makes sure everybody receives the same amount of appreciation and support from the team. It also makes sure everybody in the team is fully informed about what's going on in the team and where help could be needed. Knowing this stuff helps everybody to make better decisions. Personally, I have been part of conflicts several times so far and am absolutely sure that the solutions developed together were significantly better than the ones I could have come up with myself. In addition, we are able to make decisions that take the individual contexts into account.

Another very relevant area regarding transparency for us was and is related to our profit margins. In phase one we didn't even have profit margins on an individual level. We only had a number across everybody in the enterprise, which was a fairly useless number to base decisions on. So, we did not have a clue what projects to do and which ones to skip from a financial perspective. We were guessing. When I asked for such numbers, I was told that we didn't have them and if we had them, I couldn't see them because some people might get to know them and then use this knowledge in their salary negotiations. I couldn't even get my own numbers. To remedy this—from my perspective stupid situation if you want to make sound decisions—I started to calculate my own numbers. I knew my salary, my daily rates, and a rough estimate of the direct project costs. A number for indirect costs existed and was communicated to me. Off I went and some colleagues quickly saw the use in the numbers and adopted the calculation for themselves. Our financial officer also appreciated the idea and slowly an official calculation was provided—just to me, other area managers were kept out of the loop. We conducted a little training session in our competence area on how to deal with this sort of information and how to interpret it properly before I started sharing the numbers with every individual. We posted a chart with the area numbers on the wall (actual, trend, break-even, and goal) each month to allow self-organization around them. Everybody knew their own numbers and was updated on them every month. Once a year, we looked at everybody's numbers together in a team workshop. While this was officially forbidden because people could calculate back the salaries of their colleagues from these numbers, I found it to be a good idea, one which was appreciated by the team and deepened understanding for the matter. We started to base decisions on them: What daily rates to accept for which person, which trainings to book for whom, how many days off from customer work to allow for whom, and many more. Nobody used the numbers in their salary negotiations so far. We decided on the contrary that profit margins had to be good throughout the whole team and individual margins were not that important for us. After all, why punish a team mate for sending somebody else on a more profitable project? That didn't make sense to us. Today, individual profit margins are available for everybody inside the company and shared with most people automatically every month. "Automatically" means that—in addition to a complete overview of their teams—the competence area managers get emails for their team members from the financial tracking system and can distribute them at their discretion. From my point of view, the next step should be to send the reports to the people directly, but I expect this step to take another year.

As you can see with this example, we didn't always stick to the rules officially stated. I took a calculated risk and made it a habit to also communicate hidden agendas and background information to the team. I kept only very sensitive information secret, for example when individual people were personally affected or legal consequences might have been involved for the company. This had an amazing effect on people. Since they suddenly knew what was going on they stopped gossiping and didn't invent their own stories. They didn't even tell other colleagues throughout the enterprise. Instead, they helped the organization to achieve its goals in every way they could. It also had a great impact on trust. Knowing this kind of information made them feel appreciated and respected. It also helped them to trust me, their boss, by always showing an open hand in all our communications.

2.3.2 Performance Appraisals

This level of trust allowed us to take another big step to increase our transparency: We completely re-thought performance appraisals. In phase one every employee reported to both a department head and a competence area manager (cf. Fig. 3.2). The department head was responsible for conducting the yearly performance appraisal. However, the department head didn't know what her employees were doing because she only saw them three times a year: during the performance appraisal, at the Christmas event and during the summer party. It was ridiculous sitting there and being told: "Well, I can't really rate you, but this is my assessment of you, and by the way, this will impact your salary and your career." The session routinely continued by filling in many pages of a spreadsheet so somebody further up the command chain could compare people and decide about individuals. Later, when we had freed ourselves from the department structure (phase two), the same type of performance appraisal persisted, but it was the competence area manager conducting it. This way the person rating you at least knew what you were doing and how capable you were at it. However, it was still a one-on-one session dominated by a frenzy of spreadsheet work.

Inspired by Management 3.0's description of 360-degree-feedback (cf. Appelo, 2010) in phase three we completely ditched the established practices. We decided to conduct team workshops instead of one-on-one sessions. We used a facilitator from outside of the team to run the session so everybody could participate. Everybody prepared a flip-chart with three sections: Self-assessment, assessment by others, additional feedback (cf. Fig. 2.3).

Each person in the team had to prepare their evaluations for themselves and for the other team members in advance and bring them to the workshop. The different career levels (Junior Consultant, Consultant, Senior Consultant, Managing Consultant, Senior Managing Consultant) are already defined in terms of the expectations for each level, so it is clear to everybody what is being evaluated. We start by

Fig. 2.3 Feedback workshop chart

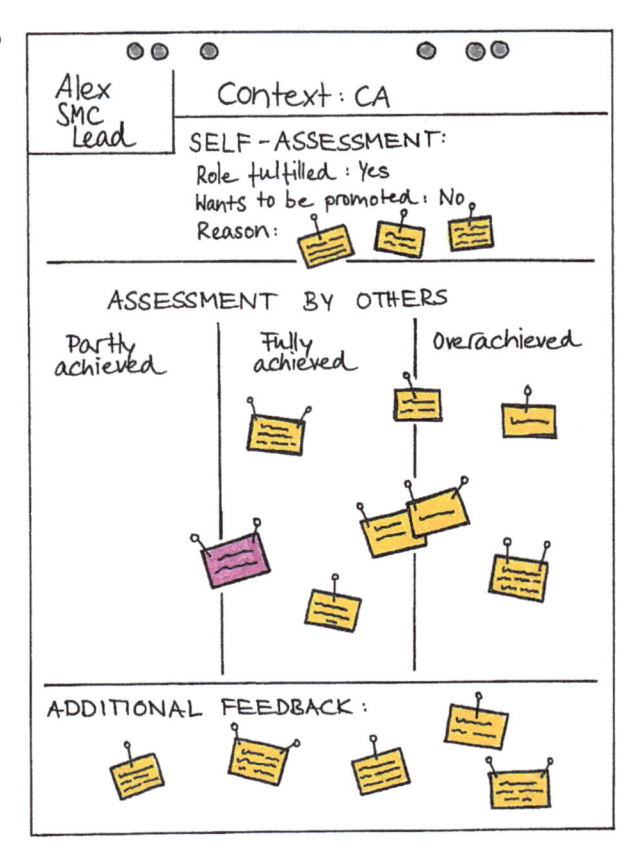

reminding everybody of the purpose and rules. Then, one by one we move round the room first asking the person being evaluated to give their own assessment of their year's activities. Once shared, everybody else then puts their sticky notes in the appropriate field to show their point of view with regard to the personal assessment. This evaluation was noted on the stickies beforehand in order to avoid spontaneous changes to individual opinions based on the now transparent group dynamic. As the boss I use a different color and am always the last to stick my notes onto the charts to avoid influencing the others. When all sticky notes are placed, we cluster around each of the charts and compare the self-assessment with the assessment by the other team members, discussing all issues openly where clarifications are needed or questions arise. If somebody disagrees with some parts of the evaluation, discussion is embraced. When all questions are answered and no further discussion is needed, we take a look at the "additional feedback" section. This feedback is not intended to be used when considering salary changes or promotions. It's purely for feedback for the team mate and strictly speaking belongs to the content of a development talk rather than to a performance appraisal workshop. However, we found it to be helpful to offer some space for additional comments. Again, questions are welcomed. Once everything is clarified, we move on to the next flip-chart and repeat the procedure. My flip-chart is the last to be reviewed to ensure that I am not negatively influenced in my assessments through the feedback I receive from the team. I don't want to "punish" anybody for their courage to give me open, honest feedback. As you see this means that the evaluation of employees and their boss indeed happens in the same workshop. At the end everybody either takes their own flip-chart with them or at least a photo of it. The competence area manager only takes photos of the upper two sections and uses this team—evaluation for decisions about money and career levels. In general, the section with the most sticky notes is the one used in the final evaluation. The manager is not bound to the team's feedback and is allowed to rate his own feedback higher than the team's. The reason for this is that there is a notable tendency in which team members try to avoid giving "bad grades" to colleagues. They prefer to choose the highest plausible column, which is often "fully achieved," for their feedback. Therefore, I still have to make the final call, because I have to not only base my assessment on where feedback is placed, but also on the written content on the notes. So far, the different evaluations matched well enough at the end of the day, so that it was not necessary for even a single down-voting of the team's appraisal by me. Had I only listened to individual feedback, this would have certainly been different.

The photo of the manager's flip-chart is also sent to the competence area manager's boss. The same procedure is repeated there. If an employee wants to escalate because she feels treated unfairly, she has four options. The first is to voice the concerns right away in the workshop so the team can validate their opinion. If the team stays with their appraisal, the employee can escalate to the competence area manager who then can decide to deviate from the team's appraisal. The third escalation option is for the employee to talk to one of our elected persons of trust. The last option is to directly talk to a member of the management board who can then try to resolve the issue. So far, we have not had a single escalation outside the team.

In my competence area, we have been living this system for several years and it still works. Other competence areas and projects (we also adopted the practice for project member appraisals) can decide to go for a different option. They can choose to do the workshop described above, make anonymous input prior to the workshop so nobody knows who gave certain feedback (this actually doesn't really work because when the discussion starts, people have to give away that they wrote something), do the feedback digitally (not a good idea either since written communication is often misinterpreted) or stay with traditional one-on-ones. It appears that over time all teams at NovaTec gravitate toward the open workshop format, but it will still take a year or two until everybody has adopted it. This is because teams need to build the necessary level of trust first. Also, we will continue to improve the approach. Next time we conduct the performance appraisal session, we want to remove the "feedback" part, because we want to clearly separate feedback from evaluation. Instead, we want to put up a section for praise, because right now we are all focusing on the last 2% that is missing to reach a specific level, which leads to the impression of not acknowledging accomplishments for some people. We are also discussing if we should do this type of workshop more than once per year.

2.3.3 Salary Distribution

The reason for us still evaluating people's individual performances is that we utterly failed at another Management 3.0 practice, namely Salary Formulas (cf. Management3.0c). The performance appraisal is needed to decide if somebody should be promoted, if a salary increase should be applied and how large it should be. So, we cannot get rid of performance appraisals if we don't find another way to distribute money across the organization. Distributing status with titles would be easy if no money was associated with it, so money is the culprit. A salary formula is intended to solve this issue by defining clear criteria, weighing them and attaching money to it. Imagine a hypothetical formula like this: Base salary depending on age, plus individual bonus based on money earned at the customer (e.g., a 30% cut) plus team bonus based on overall financial team performance (e.g., 3%). Filling it with life, it could look as follows for a consultant, age 30, who has earned a profit of 10,000€ in a team which earned a cumulated profit of 50,000€:

$$\text{base\_salary}(55{,}000€ + 30 \text{ years}^* 100€) + \text{individual\_bonus}(30\% \,^* 10{,}000€)$$
$$+ \text{team\_bonus}(3\% \,^* 50{,}000€)$$
$$= 58{,}000€ + 3000€ + 1667€ = 62{,}667€.$$

This is a very simple example to illustrate how it works. We did not actually implement it. You should be able to see the power of such an approach though: No more salary negotiations, well-described unfairness (e.g., leadership and sales efforts are not part of the formula), radical transparency. I urged the team to try it and prepared some example formulas that already were roughly balanced for our team. We established the rules that nobody would lose money if we implemented a formula and if imbalances would become obvious, we would align them over the course of several years. We even introduced the rule that one component of the formula would be the "imbalance bonus" that would be used by us to melt down disproportionate salaries with the goal to reduce this factor to zero over the course of 5–10 years. The team joyfully went along at first, thinking of additional formulas, discussing factors and inequalities. Unfortunately, when we reached the point where we should have put real numbers into the formulas for ourselves, the team chickened out. Nobody filled their own numbers in, or at least they refrained from discussing their results with the team. The idea just died. I tried to revive it half a year later, starting the process over again. As you might expect, the same story happened again. Well, you can't expect something to improve if you don't change anything, so the second fail was my mistake. We then tried an alternate approach: In one of our appraisal sessions, we inserted an additional block at the end. We placed a glass on the table for every team member and wrote one name on every glass. We were seven team mates, plus me back then. We gave 20 marbles to everybody and asked them to distribute them however they liked—they just couldn't put them into their own glasses. Every marble represented a fraction (1/140) of the available budget for salary increases even though the total amount of money was kept secret. I believed this would lead to a better impression of what the team would consider a fair distribution of money. Unfortunately, the team first refused to try the experiment. Nobody really gave a reason, but they were all reluctant to try it. Only when I told them I would make the decision anyway, if they gave me feedback or not, they slowly started to distribute the marbles. There, a pattern became apparent: First, everybody tried to put the same number of marbles into every glass. When they realized this wouldn't sum up, they started thinking with the last couple of marbles. We counted them and ended the exercise, jumping immediately into a heated conversation of why we shouldn't do something like that and openly communicate all salaries right away. Interestingly, the same people demanded both steps, which irritated me a bit. Up to this point, I considered the experiment a failure. Too many bad emotions, no team spirit and never-ending discussions without suggestions on how to reach the goal of getting the topic of money off the table for everybody. However, when I later did the maths, I realized that after deducting the evenly spread marbles from the glasses, the team result was pretty close to my own opinion I had prepared prior to the workshop. My final assessment of this exercise is that it was disaster, but not a complete disaster. I expected far more from us and overrated our maturity. The underlying issue was a different understanding of fairness though: Some people believe a fair salary is when everybody is earning the same amount of money, compared to their peer group, while others believe that money should be related to value contributed by a person. This basic conflict was triggered when distributing marbles and not knowing the baseline, the actual salary.

Later that year we had our yearly salary negotiations. Almost everybody in the team believed they were far above average and deserved a far higher pay rise than I had offered them. Even though there are many analogies to this phenomenon, for example with car drivers who also usually believe they are better drivers than the other people on the road, this came as a surprise to me, negotiating salaries for the first time. We stayed with what I had decided and nobody quit—which is an achievement in itself, I guess—but I realized that we were in dire need of a salary benchmark. Since we didn't have market data at NovaTec, I organized it. Firstly, I asked my team to elicit numbers from the headhunters calling them and share these numbers with the team. Secondly, I asked a specialized agency to provide me with numbers and lastly, I used our NovaTec-internal salary benchmark. This combination provided me with quite good numbers, chopped into salary bandwidths for different career levels.

This data was the basis for us to try a different experiment this year. We still don't share the individual salaries, neither do we share the total amount available for distribution nor the salary bandwidths for specific career levels. Our main goal is to treat everybody in a fair way, and we realized we didn't need those numbers to achieve this. The basic assumption was that salaries should be aligned with career levels. I prepared A4 sheets with the names of everybody and a line with three sections for every name. The center section always represented the current career level, the section to the left the previous lower level and the section to the right the next higher level. The first step in the workshop was for everybody to mark the "target salary" (note: not the current one!) for everybody with an "X." Nobody was allowed to talk, in order to avoid anchoring anybody. I prepared my own sheet in

Fig. 2.4 Salary workshop chart

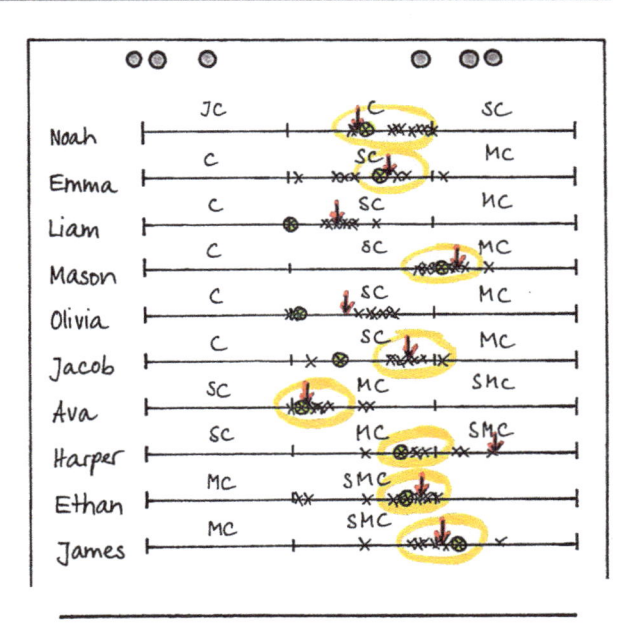

advance to make sure I also wasn't anchored by the team. When everybody was done, we copied the information from the charts onto a flip-chart (cf. Fig. 2.4).

Each person's own evaluation was marked with a red arrow. Then, we moved through the chart, person by person. We noticed the clusters, differences, and spread. If the person wanted to ask a question, they were free to. Usually, people wanted to know who were the outliers on both sides and why. In all cases, the team mates were happy to come forward and offer explanations, even though this was completely voluntary. When this discussion subsided, I added my own prepared opinion (green X). In most cases this matched nicely, but in some cases, there was a difference. Since I knew the team's opinion on salary and performance, I now could reevaluate my own opinion.

For the cases with closely clustered opinions, we circled the cluster. This symbolized to the employee that the target salary would be somewhere in this cluster. The workshop only took 1 h and ended with me acknowledging to sleep it over. Three days after the workshop, I decided on the salaries and actually changed my mind in two cases, based on the team's feedback. Knowing the target salaries, I now could compare it to the actual salaries and distribute my budget accordingly. Some people received small raises, some received high raises, and one person actually received no increase. I have to say making the choice was much easier than in previous years since my confidence in finding a fair solution for everybody was increased through this workshop. When I communicated the salaries to everybody in one-on-one sessions, they only took 5–15 min and everybody was content with the results. Overall, the experience was very positive for everybody.

2.4 Establishing Values

Only one person complained. This person had never been with another employer and was accustomed to high yearly raises at NovaTec in the past. He is an exceptional employee and developed quickly during the last years, that's why his salary was always aligned with his value to the enterprise. Unfortunately, this employee now considered a certain percentage in yearly salary increases as normal. Even though this person came in second in absolute numbers, he scored lowest in satisfaction. He did not understand that the more you earn, the larger a certain percentile of your salary actually becomes in absolute terms, leading to an exponential curve if you try to match a certain percentage year after year. With the increased transparency, I now hope his stance will shift by the time we reach next year's workshop. In addition, I will also continue to focus on a salary formula. This would help tremendously in setting expectations. Doing this without the team's support though is not something I want to progress.

2.4 Establishing Values

For me, the most frustrating aspect of failing at the salary question was that we built our team on the foundation of strong values and violated several of them there. It's not about pinning some nice sounding words up on the wall and hoping for the best, we actually share our values and emphasize them every day. When we started in phase two to actively work our way into Management 3.0, one of the first experiments we chose was working with values. There were no company values at the time. Management 3.0 advocates to distinguish between "core values" and "wish values" (cf. Fig. 2.5). Core values are the ones you already practice, wish values are the ones you want to improve or adopt. We conducted a short workshop, pinning the example values from "#Workout" (the book was discontinued and replaced by "Managing for Happiness," cf. Appelo, 2016) to a whiteboard. Each of us then chose his top five core values, focusing on the top three in the next step. Of course, some of us chose values not represented on the whiteboard, but that was fine. We clustered them and asked ourselves if we had stories from our working life that would actually back up the claim that these were already practiced core values. Plenty of stories followed and we dot-voted to come up with four values: Professionalism, openness, transparency, and "we never walk alone." The last one is

Fig. 2.5 Our competence area values

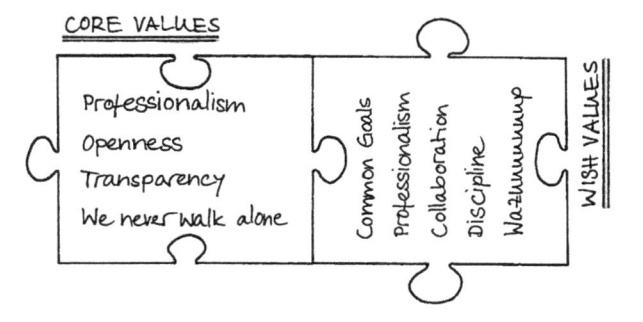

interesting because it was our top-voted one and not part of the Management 3.0 values list. It is our primary focus as a team: to help each other out whenever needed.

We repeated the exercise for our wish values and came up with collaboration, professionalism, discipline, and common goals. Collaboration was aiming at actively working with several team members in the same project, which is rare for us. Professionalism was represented both as a core and a wish value because our view was that we were more professional than anybody else at NovaTec, but not professional enough to compete with the big shots in the market. One main reason for that was missing discipline in tasks we didn't like, which is unfortunately still the case from time to time. Common goals highlighted the fact that we still had a vision and a strategy from phase one, but most team members were not part of the team back then and thus had not been involved in the creation. We remedied this shortly after by creating an updated vision and strategy. As you can see, we used value stories again to illustrate what we were talking about.

Once we had agreed on our core and wish values, we printed them out and hung them up in our team room, right above our main whiteboard. From that point on we made reference to our values every day and deeply ingrained them into everything we do together. The only thing we still have to do to complete the value practices is writing down our value stories and creating a culture book. A culture book is a collection of our values and the corresponding stories that allows everybody reading it to understand what we are talking about. A culture book can be very colorful and fun to read and we do want to create one, but we didn't prioritize it highly enough so far. It's still in the backlog.

The values exercise motivated us to take a closer look at the topic of identity symbols (cf. Management3.0d). Identity symbols are logos, phrases, colors, or anything else that are associated with your team, business unit, or company. While we did have a company logo and t-shirts, we did not have anything that was representative for our team. So we started looking for a symbol and a friendly comic designer created a symbol for us: A superhero, carrying a futuristic torch, and two spheres representing our agile consulting products and the "light" this brings to our customers. It looked awesome and I put it on the sign next to the door to our team room, and also into our internal wiki system. While nobody in the team complained, nobody cheered either. The idea sort of passed away. Some time later we discussed the topic of identity symbols again and found out that nobody could really identify with a superhero. But since no one had a better idea at the time, nobody had complained. We started a new initiative, but nothing cool came to our minds. Then, one morning I stumbled over a new value pinned next to our wish values above the whiteboard. It read "WAZUUUUUUUP." I was surprised and didn't have the slightest clue what this meant. My team mates laughed and showed me an old Budweiser commercial. It became a meme for us, being used excessively for months. While it certainly opposed our value of professionalism to stick out your tongue and shout "WAZUUUUUUUP," it was a unique identifier for this team. It became an identity symbol for some time. After about half a year, the tongues stayed in again and people used the term "fun" instead. The reason is that our vision became so compelling for everybody that the vision morphed into our identity symbol. Right now two members of the team are designing t-shirts with our vision on them—in their private time, willing to pay for them themselves. This was my key learning from this failed experiment: You cannot mandate identity symbols. You can offer resources, you can nudge the idea, but the initiative must come from the team.

Another way we used our values is with our praise system, Kudo Cards (cf. Management3.0e). Kudo Cards are colorful cards you can use to say "thank you" to somebody. They are a way to deliver instant recognition. When we started experimenting with Management 3.0, Kudo Cards was the first practice we introduced. We looked at the website, printed out the cards and just went for it. We did not ask any critical questions or wonder if everybody would get their "fair share of praise." We just started courageously. We placed a stack of printed and cut cards on a sideboard in our team room and waited to see what would happen. As the team's manager I wanted to lead by example and tried to write some cards every week. This led to a problem: Where should I place the written cards? Without a better option, I handed them directly to the recipients. They smiled—and shared that we could improve the whole experience by also introducing a kudo box. A kudo box is a box you can use to put the Kudo Cards in and then open it publicly at a certain point in time, unleashing a mass of kudos. Within a couple of days, such a box magically appeared in the team room. We used it, and then thought further about when to open it for maximum effect. Reading into the Management 3.0 practice, we wanted to do it publicly and trustingly. Since we organize ourselves around Scrum, we chose our monthly Sprint Review meeting to open the box and read out the cards to the team and all stakeholders present at that moment. Again, we did not ask any of the "what if" questions like "What if a card is negative and your boss hears it in the Review?" We just trusted each other to handle such a potential incident professionally should it arise.

The impact was tremendous. Suddenly, all our stakeholders, including the management board, wanted to write cards as well. We taught them how to use them, had a larger amount printed on better quality paper, and distributed the cards in hallways and offices all over the company. At first, we didn't notice anything happening. We thought the mental barrier to trying something new had stopped them from experimenting. So, we focused on our own team and discussed what to do with the Kudo Cards now that we had received them in the Review meeting. We decided for maximum transparency to place them on the outward facing side of our team room door. All cards landed there, shouting out to the world whatever the card proclaimed. Within a couple of months, the door wasn't big enough to hold all cards, so we started using the adjacent wall as well (cf. Fig. 2.6).

A month after we had distributed the Kudo Cards across the company, we found some in our kudo box that did not come from our own team. In addition, we found some that were written by the team, but were addressing people outside the team. We kept our approach, read them out in the Sprint Review and handed them over to the recipients or hung them up on our door/wall display when they were for one of our team.

People liked that. They liked that a lot. Every single card we handed over to anybody ended up on a door, a computer screen, or an office wall. This was the spark

Fig. 2.6 Our Kudo Wall

other teams needed and it caught on. Today, this practice is used by about half the company. Some employees even introduced a digital version of this in our internal wiki.

We extended the practice by combining it with our values. Whenever we write a Kudo Card now, we add a hashtag and the corresponding value to it (cf. Fig. 2.7).

People can choose any value they like for the hashtag (or don't use it at all), it is not mandatory to use one of our defined values. This gives us an impression of what values are actually valued in our team. Interestingly, it's mostly our core and wish values—but every month there are several Kudo Cards with deviating values as well. It is a self-reinforcing way to deal with values.

Kudo cards are a well-established practice at our company today. Even after several years, nothing negative has happened—nobody felt treated unfairly, the tool wasn't used in an inappropriate way, and the acceptance is growing further every day. When facilitating Management 3.0 workshops, I often meet people who fear something bad could happen due to these cards. In our experience, this is a logical but rather academic threat. We have not encountered such effects in practice, neither

Fig. 2.7 Example Kudo Card

in our own team nor at customers. If you are worrying, my advice is to run an experiment and just try it.

The last experiment we tried with values was to introduce a tool called Bonusly (cf. https://bonus.ly). The idea of using hashtags was actually borrowed from there. Bonusly is a tool intended to distribute micro-bonuses. Every team member gets a certain amount of virtual credits (we called ours "Novas") at the first day of each month. These credits can be awarded to another team member by sending a message via the system, mentioning the amount of Novas, the name of the recipient(s), and a note what these credits are awarded for. If you don't spend all your credits in 1 month, whatever you didn't spend is lost and everybody starts with the same number of distributable Novas again the next month. Whatever Novas you are awarded go to your vault and remain there forever until you spend them on something. Bonusly's idea is to translate these points to small sums of money or to couple them with a HR cafeteria system, e.g. using the credits on a sports club membership, a movie voucher or something similar. In our team, we didn't like this idea because it translates to providing extrinsic motivation. We don't want people to show appreciation for each other so they can go to the movies. We want people to show appreciation for each other so they can feel recognized. Therefore, we altered the system and inserted our own rewards (cf. Fig. 2.8). For example, Christian offered to bake muffins for a small amount of Novas. Or you could book a private workout session with Boris, our tough mudder athlete.

This system worked well for some time. It was something new, it was fun, and there were muffins! Unfortunately, after some time people stopped using it for several months, and then suddenly started to use it again. So far we are not certain what happened. One theory is that it is natural for such systems to be used intensively sometimes and not at all at other times. Another theory is that a tool that is fully digital is less interesting than a physical communication like a Kudo Wall. After all, once you received the Bonusly message, it flows down in the recognition list and you have to actively scroll down a page or two if you want to see it again later. On top of that, you need to open the website to use it, something that needs your personal

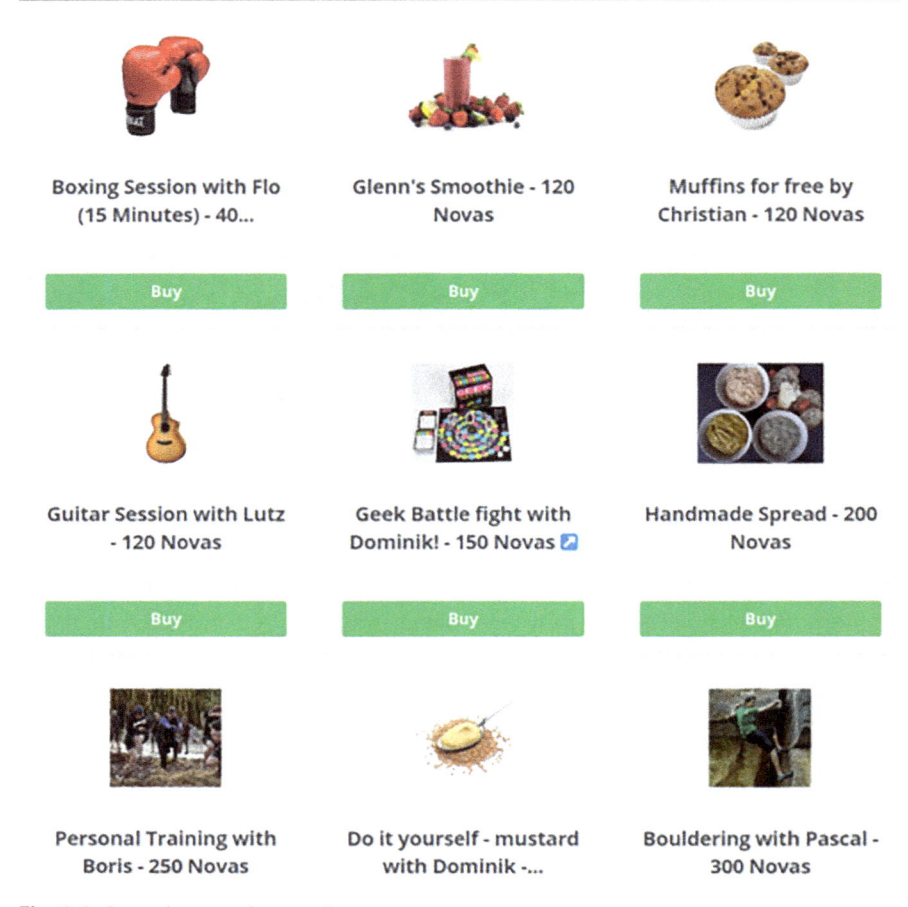

Boxing Session with Flo (15 Minutes) - 40...	Glenn's Smoothie - 120 Novas	Muffins for free by Christian - 120 Novas
Buy	Buy	Buy
Guitar Session with Lutz - 120 Novas	Geek Battle fight with Dominik! - 150 Novas	Handmade Spread - 200 Novas
Buy	Buy	Buy
Personal Training with Boris - 250 Novas	Do it yourself - mustard with Dominik -...	Bouldering with Pascal - 300 Novas

Fig. 2.8 Bonusly example rewards

action. As I said, we don't know the reasons so far. In the same time span, the use of Kudo Cards went up and down as well, but not as dramatically as with Bonusly. We will continue to watch it and use both systems.

2.5 Hiring and Firing

The most significant change in procedures to support team maturity was in hiring and firing team members. In phase one, only members of the management board hired and fired people. While specific members of the competence areas were involved, the board made the decisions. Regular team members were not involved. Since management only looked for specific skills (remember me being told I wasn't a programmer), it was coincidence if people fit into teams or not.

In phase two, we turned this upside down. While only in phase three the actual power to hire somebody moved to the competence area managers, we already did the practical hiring decisions in the team. No matter if somebody applies from outside or inside the company, they undergo the same procedure. First, I take a look at their cover letters and CVs. We do not look carefully for high grades or job references. If there is a remote hint for passion regarding agile methods, we invite the person to an interview. We don't want to hire CVs—we want to hire people.

The first interview is usually just with me as the competence area manager. I verify their competence in agile methods, check for travel preferences, salaries, and motivation. If one or several of these points don't fit, I provide feedback to the applicant and advise her that we are not able to come together at this point in time. If it looks like a good fit, we invite the person (sometimes on the same day) to get to know the team. For us that means 3–5 h intense collaboration with the applicant, asking all sorts of questions about agility, Scrum, and other stuff. What we are really looking for is not fluency in the agile topic, it is conformity with our values and a strong urge to learn. After the interview, we ask the applicant to leave the team alone for 15–20 min. In this timeframe, we draw a grid up on the whiteboard, listing our (and the company) values, adding the questions how long it will take until the applicant can be placed at a customer, and how long it will take until she will be profitable for the team and company. Then each of us puts their opinion onto the board, we briefly discuss it, make the decision (the team has the right to reject any candidate, as well as I do), and then we ask the applicant to join us again. We share our feedback and explain what it means for us. If we don't see that our values are shared to some extent, we thank the applicant for her time and ask her to leave. If the values are there but the person can't be engaged at the customer early, we explain what this means in terms of our expectation toward her learning curve and commitment to grow. At this point, we are usually willing to invest in the person. We tell her that we would love to have her in our team and ask her to consider it overnight. If the applicant signs up, we jointly create a development plan for the next couple of months and help her to reach our expectations that always correspond with her salary level.

People tend to appreciate this level of commitment to potential new employees. Even some of the people we reject come back to us after the interview and thank us for the thorough and candid feedback. When I am on holiday and applicants are planned to come and meet the team, I fully delegate this to the team. In these cases, I waive my right to veto the decisions and they can make the decision without me.

However, we experienced two problems with this procedure, whether I am on vacation or not. The first is that some people are overwhelmed by our expectations and turn us down after the interview. While this is generally a good thing (we don't want people in the team who don't want to be in the team), we still spent half a day with the full team getting to know this person. Right now we are trying to be more strict in the first face to face interview to filter these applicants out early. The second problem has to do with our maturity level as a team. While saying "yes" to an applicant is easy, saying "no" is not. Especially since most people in the team are very people-oriented with a strong urge to help others, they don't use the word "no."

This makes it difficult for me to recognize when they want to use their veto option. For example, we had an applicant during my last vacation. We decided on a stand-in and he did the first interview via telephone. The feedback after the call was not "no, we rejected him," it was "Dominik, you should talk to this person as well." So I had to talk to the applicant as well only to find out that he didn't really fit into the team. When I had rejected him and talked to my stand-in about it, he told me that he also believed him to be a bad fit. I asked why he hadn't said so and saved all of us a useless interview. He responded that it had taken him a day or two to reach that conclusion, based on thinking beyond the candidates immediately obvious strong agile background. For me, this was a bad excuse, because there were 2 weeks between his interview and mine—more than enough time to cancel it. It wasn't the first time when it dawned on me that "no" wasn't part of this team's interview language. Today, I am very carefully listening to what people say when asked about their opinion. If it's not a clear "yes," people actually want to tell me "no" without having to tell the applicant. It's something we are constantly working on.

Firing people is more difficult, of course. It was and is not common at NovaTec to fire people. People are demoted instead, if their performance doesn't match their positions and they continuously fail to improve. Unfortunately, sometimes this isn't good enough and we learned it the hard way.

In Germany, when you enter a company there is a law protecting you after 6 months in office. It is tough to fire somebody afterwards, even if there are good business reasons. If you want to fire somebody for personal reasons, you have to send that person written warnings several times before you are legally safe. Within these 6 months, employees are not protected. Therefore, it is normal in Germany to use these 6 months as a probation period. In our team, we make the "keep or fire" decision together in a quick round, similar to what I described above. Usually, people make it without problem or even hesitation. Just one time it went badly.

We had a colleague who was very quick in talking but very slow in learning. He failed massively several times both at customers and internally and we constantly tried to coach him toward better performance. The pattern was always the same: Something blew up in our faces, we discussed it with our colleague, he promised improvements and all sorts of action. Later he reported on having performed these actions. Then, the next thing blew up in our faces. Since we had the impression that he was seriously trying to improve, we didn't fire him within the first 6 months. Only after this time we found out that he had constantly lied to us: He had only done a fraction of the promised actions, his customers were so unhappy that they called me (sheesh, why didn't they call earlier—we trusted the reports of our colleague and didn't call them ourselves...). We even had evidence that he had lied during his application concerning some important facts. When we fired him, we had to choose between paying money for more legal investigations or paying money to get rid of him quickly. We decided for the latter option.

This fail taught us a valuable lesson: Not everybody on this planet shares the same understanding of honor and commitment as we do. After this event, we became much more cautious and didn't tolerate as much deviation anymore. While we would love to not have to do this, we are scarred by that event.

2.6 Learnings

Building teams is not easy. As you have read, we have tried many different things, which all play together hand-in-hand. The result is a truly fantastic team. Every single member of this team says that they have never experienced such a great team before, and that they don't want to miss out on it. This reflects in how we behave toward each other, how we deal with conflicts, how quickly help is available, and of course how productive we are. This is the result of a pinch of good luck, and a huge pile of work. While you cannot force a group of people to grow into a team, you can do your part and provide the necessary environment. To focus your learning, here are my key insights on building teams, gathered both in failure and success:

A first step for building teams is to get to know each other. For me this means working together in workshops, sharing personal stories and backgrounds, being a role model by putting yourself out there too, and using every possible opportunity to engage with the team, for example at a Christmas party. The Management 3.0 practice of personal maps is very useful in structuring this approach. Also, enjoying frequent team events together, and having them organized by the team itself, for example by a "chief fun officer," all helps bring people closer together.

All this builds trust. However building trust requires more than just getting to know each other. It requires allowing mistakes and showing your own mistakes as well. Conflicts will arise. When they do, don't use email to resolve them, talk directly to people instead. When you resolve problems in the team together, trust increases. If you can't abstain from using email, try the Management 3.0 practice of feedback wraps to structure your message. Also learn more about your team mates by using Moving Motivators (also a Management 3.0 practice), because every person has different intrinsic motivators, which is one major root cause for difference of opinion, misunderstandings, and conflict. Above all, transparency is paramount for trust.

If you want to create self-organized teams, consider a radical approach on transparency. Discuss all problems openly in the team. Open your books and let your team know about their financial performance. Explain hidden agendas and background information, as long as it doesn't damage the company. Do away with individual performance appraisals. If you can't for some reason, try to conduct team workshops for this type of appraisal instead. Try to introduce a public salary formula (a Management 3.0 practice), but do not expect people to behave rationally when talking about money. Maybe this is a topic that is beyond democratic ruling once imbalances are present. At least it requires a very high maturity level of the people involved.

The basis from which a team should act is not the company or education. It is strong and shared values. A beautiful way to come to a conclusion here is described in Management 3.0's value stories and culture books. They are very powerful. If you don't push it and you are lucky, you might even see your team establishing and using their own identity symbols. Once you established your values, use every opportunity to reinforce them. Talk about them in every meeting you conduct, relate to them in every decision you make, and write them on Kudo Cards (a Management 3.0

practice) with a hashtag so everybody realizes that living your own values earns you recognition. You can also try this with other tools like Bonusly, although for us Kudo Cards rule.

Last but not least, you must change the hiring and firing procedures if you want your team to stay intact over a longer period of time. Only if you involve your team deeply in such decisions and also allow them to veto your own ideas will you be able to maintain the team's spirit. Be careful though: Your team might feel uncomfortable with saying "no" or firing people. If this is the case, you will still have to make this kind of decision yourself and read between the lines of what your team mates tell you. Alternatively, you can ask them in one-on-one interviews.

Changing Organizational Structure 3

Once you have established a well-functioning team with a high level of trust, you will inevitably start thinking about your organizational structure. Whether you actually change something however is a different story of course. We changed quite a lot on different levels at different points in time. The following chapters will look briefly at the changes conducted inside the competence area of agile methods, dive deeply into organization-wide changes, throw a glance at the way we set up satellite sites, and finally discuss how to excel at virtual working.

3.1 Changes Within One Area

In phase one, we were bound to the then existing rules and had to live within them. Our competence area (CA) of "agile methods and processes" consisted of one competence area manager, one competence group leader, and myself (cf. Fig. 3.1). In this setup, the best description for my role was "ordinary worker." I do not know why it was set up in this way.

There were no additional people in this setup. All three of us were involved in customer engagements: The competence area manager as project manager in a non-agile environment, the competence group leader as Scrum Master in a single semi-agile context, and myself as Professional Scrum Trainer and agile coach in several enterprises. We quickly found that this chain of hierarchy didn't help us grow the business unit. We also found that quite often the competence group leader and myself argued ferociously with the CA manager. All our energies were channeled on inner-area conflicts. We tried to get out of this struggle by conducting a series of strategy workshops. The outcome was mediocre, but what we did achieve was that we eliminated the role of competence group leader.

In phase two, we went further. At that point in time, I had accepted the role of competence area manager and we had grown to seven people. We had stayed with the idea of not introducing competence group leaders. Instead, we were focusing on cross-functional teams without specific areas of expertise. It was unimaginable for us

Fig. 3.1 Phase one competence area structure

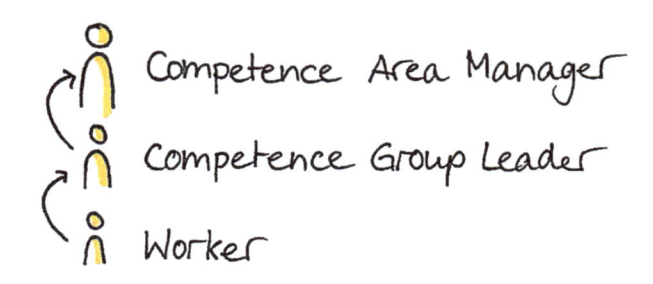

Competence Area Manager
Competence Group Leader
Worker

to divide ourselves in experts for Scrum Mastery, Product Ownership, Kanban, and so forth. We deeply believe that a good agile coach must be an expert in all these competencies—and more. We continued with further flattening hierarchies. While we couldn't really remove more layers, we could change the way we worked with them. We try to interact on a level playing field. This manifests in our team members making decisions without fearing reprimands by anybody. Every peanut was discussed at board level, no matter how large the sum of money involved. People feared the effort and consequently didn't file requests, if they could help it. Today, we discuss and decide such things, for example education expenses, within the team. If somebody wants to book a course, they just discuss it with the team and the team allocates the budget. Management just trusts us to act professionally.

This level playing field is also enacted in all other aspects of our competence area's management. In most cases I see my role as equal to the team, being a regular team member most of the time. Only on rare occasions I have to put my "boss" hat on and decide things the team cannot or does not want to decide themselves. One of our main mantras is: "Don't ask for permission, ask for forgiveness." While I would appreciate some colleagues to actually ask for forgiveness a tiny bit more often, this system generally works very well. You can read more about it in Sect. 9.1.

One argument that is often brought up by people visiting us and learning about the way we operate is one of size. Some people do not believe that the way we operate scales. As a business unit, we are still small enough to act as a single team while others in some cases have to manage 50 employees or more. We do not have a good answer for this question yet. We grew from 3 people to 12 right now. This growth worked with our structure. We are approaching a point where we won't be able to sustain our single-team structure. Our idea right now is to work with several cross-functional teams, sharing a joint Sprint Planning and a joint Sprint Review meeting, working independently outside those meetings. This way of working should theoretically function up to a hundred employees. However, we have not fully piloted it yet. We will blog about it once we have learnings to share.

Another aspect of local structure is the question who should be part of this structure at all. Most articles and discussions about structure focus very much on a technical view that draws some bubbles and boxes on a chart. However, any organizational structure must serve the people using it, as well as the organization providing it. For me this means we cannot put a structure that is made for a different type of employee than the ones we have to good use. Organizations with a long history tend to develop a strong organizational culture that either assimilates or weeds out everybody who is not yet belonging to the culture. This automatically leads to a "good fit" of employees and structure, until the organization as such perishes. In our case, we didn't have that luxury. We wanted to change the existing organizational culture, we did not want to be devoured by it. Therefore, we had to choose a different approach. We defined some key elements of the team culture we wanted to have, such as our values, a common goal, and a definition of what you, as a team member, need to know in different domains. All this was new to NovaTec at the time and deviated vastly from the existing culture. Then we applied these elements with vigor in our competence area. This led to some people not wanting to be part of the team. It felt too uncomfortable for them. We demanded a lot from everybody and in turn generated things like team spirit, which some of them had never asked for. In some cases, we urged people to leave the team or didn't let them in the first place. To put it bluntly, we removed incompatible employees from our team instead of defining a suboptimal but common and lulling organizational structure. Today, nobody is still part of the team who preferred a hierarchical structure or a state excluding ownership and accountability for normal team members. Other areas of NovaTec are adopting similar approaches step by step.

3.2 Bigger Changes

Taking a look at the bigger picture in phase one shows that we had a fairly complicated organizational structure (cf. Fig. 3.2).

Every employee had to fulfill the needs of several roles at NovaTec: Competence group leaders and competence area managers demanded technical support and personal growth, project managers asked for commitment in the project one was working in, department heads were doing the performance appraisals, and the members of the management board in many cases went directly to employees if they wanted something. To further complicate matters, most people filling these roles were not trained for it and therefore were unable to fulfill them as defined. That is, if something was defined at all, which was only the case for the minority of roles. This spider web of demands at the end of the day made it impossible for an employee to know what to do in order to earn more money or get promoted. So, people barricaded themselves into their projects and tried to mainly ignore all other demands. Of course, if you see your project context at the customer's site as your primary obligation, you are very likely to switch jobs if this customer offers you one. This is what happened. When we tried to untangle this mess in phase three, we started with removing the department head role. Most of these people didn't know what their assigned employees were doing all day anyways, and employee feedback regarding this role was the worst. We defined their duties and tried to match them with names. This failed since we didn't have the right people on board. We looked further and noticed that we had another role predestined to also cover the duties of department heads: the competence area manager. Most of them were actually able to

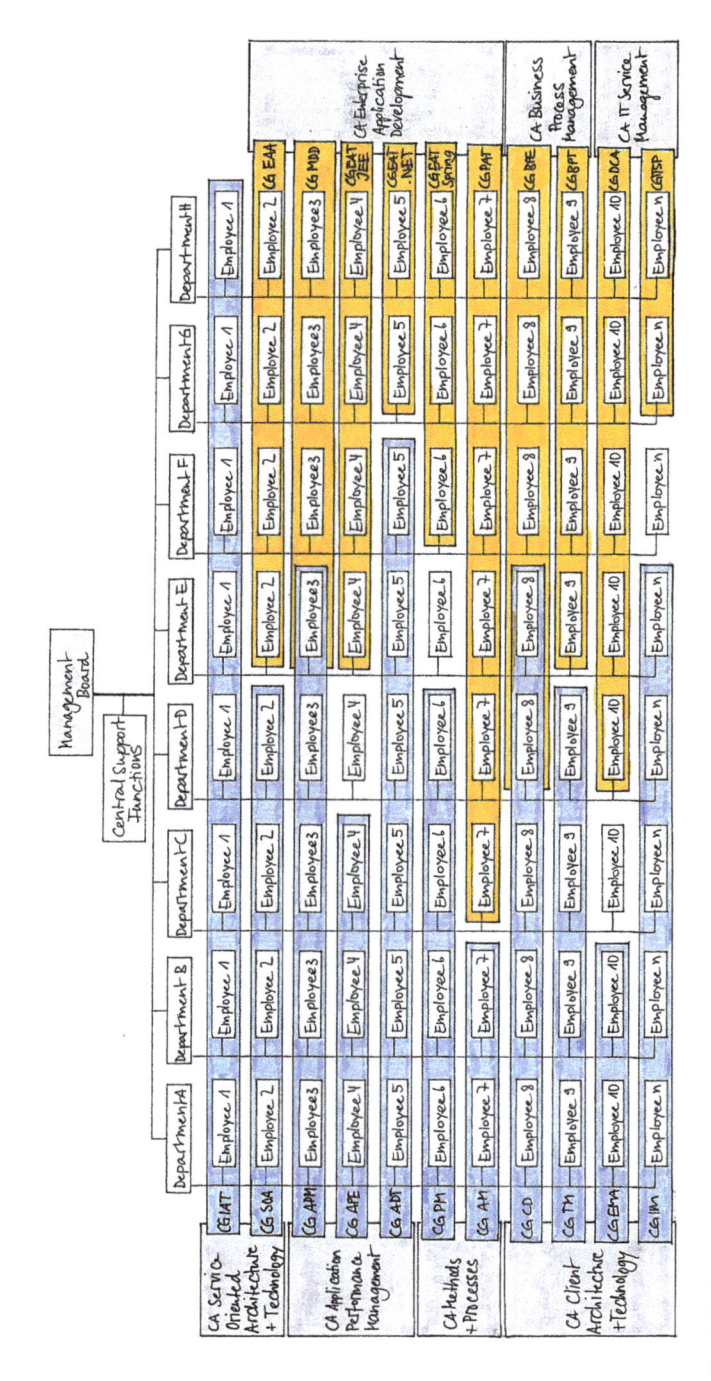

Fig. 3.2 Original organizational structure

3.2 Bigger Changes

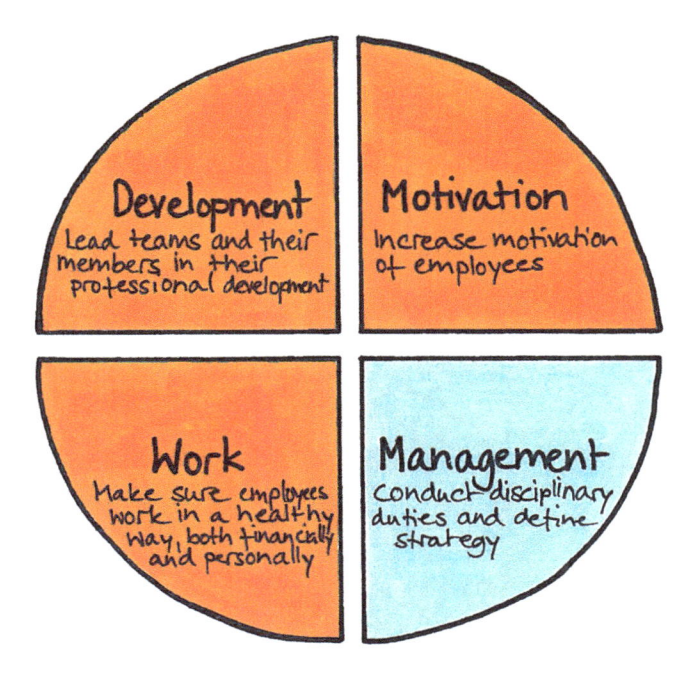

Fig. 3.3 Competence area manager duties

fulfill the duties of a department head. We quickly defined the competence area manager role (cf. Fig. 3.3).

CA managers were now officially accountable for everything they had done anyway so far: Lead their teams in their professional development, increase motivation of employees and make sure they work in a healthy way, both financially and personally. All these could also be delegated, but we refrained from defining a specific role for it. It is fine for a CA manager to delegate something to the whole team, or delegate it to an individual, whether they hold a particular title or not. This massively relieved pressure from the competence group leader role. We also enlarged the competence area manager role by attaching strategical obligations and the duties of a department head to it: Accountability for disciplinary management. These last two areas cannot be delegated; the CA manager must fulfill them himself.

Now, with the department heads removed and competence area managers clarified, we moved our attention to the structure and purpose of competence areas. In phase one, departments were just randomly chosen storage basins for employees living in projects. Today, departments no longer exist and competence areas are largely autonomous value-creation units. While NovaTec still earns money by renting employees to customers and offering consulting services, the competence areas are now accountable for their own profitability and their overall contribution to NovaTec (which can as well be something other than money). The decision to hire or fire somebody is made here now, while up to phase two this decision was made by

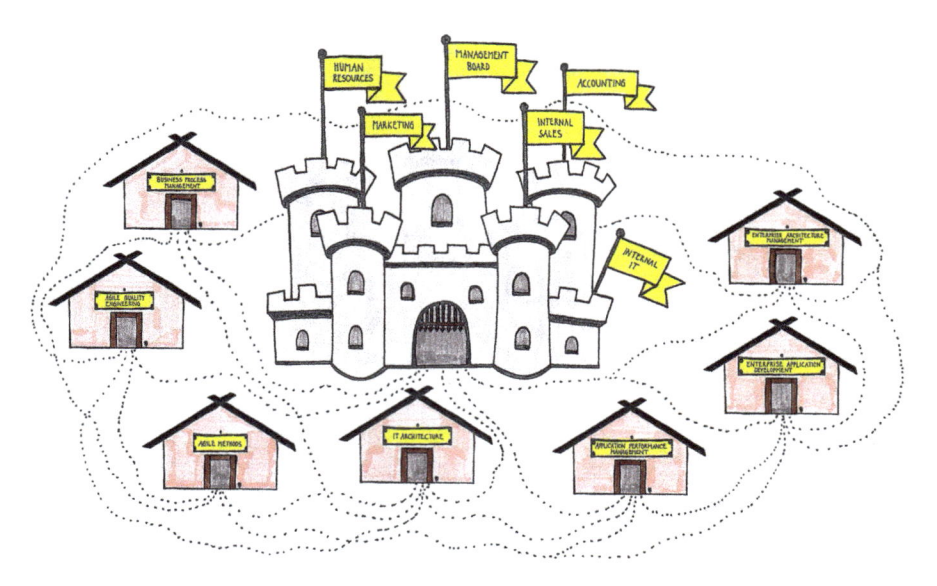

Fig. 3.4 Value creation units with a dominant central authority

the members of the management board. Also, strategies primarily applying to the competence areas are now established and account for the different requirements of the differing functional topics in the market. This level of autonomy gives our organizational structure a more organic feel, because there is not really a hierarchy anymore (cf. Fig. 3.4).

Having said all this, there are a couple of central functions that are still dominant and considered "must-use" in the organization. This applies to marketing, internal sales, accounting, human resources, internal IT and—last but not least—the management board. My personal assessment is that this situation will change next. Marketing cannot effectively work with seven different strategies and a multitude of simultaneous demands and therefore must be completely moved into the competence areas or become a strictly focused support function.

Internal sales will have to meet a similar fate. Sales pitches as well as the contents of offers are already done by the competence areas today. It is impossible for an internal sales agent to stay on top of seven different product portfolios with various specialties that only apply to one or two competence areas. This leads to dissatisfaction on all sides, which brings me to my estimation that all operative sales tasks will move completely into the units within the next 2 years.

Our human resources department is a different kettle of fish. Today they are primarily doing legal stuff and fulfilling the demands of the competence areas. Personnel innovations are coming from the competence area managers and from individual employees, such as our "happiness officer." In terms of Agility and change, our HR department is insignificant. From an organizational structure point of view, this is actually positive, because it means nothing has to change for them. They will probably stay a central unit, now and in the future.

The most difficult assessment is our internal IT department. They provide us with important infrastructure such as computers, tools, printers, and so on. It definitely makes sense to have these services in a central unit. A major risk in my opinion is that they potentially might be too slow in providing their services to the competence areas in the future. My gut feeling is that the IT department will have to undergo major change within the next couple of years to keep up with the change in the rest of the organization.

Major change is also relevant for the members of the management board. They are already in the middle of it. In phase one and earlier, their primary task was to micromanage. For the smallish company NovaTec was back then, this was all right, but today it is no longer appropriate. Also, leadership style and the level of delegation are changing dramatically, which requires a completely new way of thinking and a brand-new set of skills. In terms of organizational structure, there is a switch from "kings" at the top of the pyramid to "connectors," still making strategical decisions but making sure the right people are talking to each other at the right point in time so these people can make the right decisions for everything else. This means the board became a value-unit like the competence areas and the other departments as well. To illustrate this a little bit more vividly, imagine what would happen if management started to make a series of bad decisions or to plague the competence areas with abysmal leadership. The areas are autonomous: They would break with NovaTec and work for themselves or just ignore management. Ignoring management actually is the equivalent of letting the "management" value-unit die.

The current structure is allowing for rapid creation or dissolution of value-units. This is actually very positive, because it is quite easy to create an environment for new ideas—or to let ideas die again. If we realize that a new idea has potential and we also have some people who want to explore it, we no longer need somebody from a central authority to take a look at it from within biased central structures. We now can just create a new competence area with their own structures, strategies, and ideas. This allows for much more efficient and accurate assessments of new opportunities in the market. Of course, when the idea proves not to be feasible, the competence area can be disbanded again, moving the people to other areas instead of having to fire them. This keeps competence in the enterprise. In phases one and two, NovaTec was big at failing with some of our new ideas due to a dysfunctional decision structure in the management board. For example, we established an office in Jeddah, Saudi Arabia. Unfortunately, we didn't know the market well and didn't have a transparent strategy on what to sell there to whom. We accumulated losses for several years and only after the members of the management board had changed, was the office closed. The process of closing it was difficult and painful. From my point of view, the whole story was a total management disaster.

Another—slightly better—example was the competence area of "data center automation." We had the idea to create a software product for this purpose and just did it. Unfortunately, nobody had researched the market and thus nobody knew that there were already other players focusing on this task much more intensely with more than a hundred times our investment. This fact became obvious to us at a sales pitch when the customer asked us how we positioned ourselves compared to specific other products. Our team then started to do some market research, and discovered the extent of the competition, but for the same reasons as in the example above, management still kept the lights on. Only after we had accumulated losses for several years and realized that we wouldn't get beyond a total of two customers in the foreseeable future, was the product stopped. This time, disbanding the structures was much easier, because we could just close the competence area and move the people to another one. Unfortunately, this still produced a mess because we still had weak leadership in place. All of the affected employees were frustrated, some of them left even though serious efforts were undertaken by management to keep them on board. Again, a management failure, but not as big as the one before. From my point of view, we are improving in failing, which is a very important skill in the agile world. Today, we should be even better at it, because we have put the right people in leadership positions and have improved our leadership skills significantly. We will know for sure when the next idea fails.

The key players in this new structure are the competence area managers with their teams. They create business success with their strategies, they help employees to enjoy their tenure at NovaTec through their leadership skills, and they cooperate closely to make sure the whole construct works together. They are also the primary source for organizational innovation at NovaTec.

In phase one, the CA managers were primarily people being better informed by management than their CA members. They couldn't really make decisions, these were made by the members of the management board. In phase three, this has changed completely. Now it is the CA managers who make decisions (in many cases together with their teams) and it is the management board which is informed. Competence area managers are now empowered and activate their full potential. Decision-making is more decentralized, which usually leads to better decisions. This is an ongoing activity and we are still learning from doing. Sometimes decisions don't acknowledge all the information available to members of the board, and sometimes managers are trying to make decisions they were used to making but shouldn't be doing so today. We are still at the beginning of the learning curve. What we are noticing already is a steep increase in employee happiness and in operative margins. While this cannot be attributed to any single change described in this book and certainly not to simply changing the organizational structure, the latter had an above-average impact for sure. These changes were the fertilizer for growing teams, establishing trust and making better decisions. These changes were the preconditions necessary to develop autonomy and purpose, which again is a considerable part of the basis for employee intrinsic motivation (cf. Pink, 2011).

3.3 Satellite Sites

As you saw in the previous chapter, satellite sites received some attention at NovaTec. The concept changed fundamentally within the last years and is still not perfectly finalized. When I joined NovaTec, we had three branch offices: Munich, Frankfurt, and Jeddah, Saudi Arabia. My impression was that there was no strategy in place, neither for the creation of new branch offices nor for the individual sites. The result was that creating branches was an act of favoritism of individuals living there, the growth and development of specific sites appeared to be a result of coincidence.

As described in Sect. 3.2, Jeddah turned out to be disastrous. In the aftermath of phase two, we also screwed up in Berlin. When we redefined the department head role to be merged with the competence area manager role, we didn't consider what would happen to our branch office managers in Munich, Frankfurt, and Berlin, who until then were disciplinarily responsible for people at those locations. We didn't even involve them (or the employees working there) at all. The worst thing is that we didn't just forget them—we actively decided not to include them. This led to understandable reactions by these people. They had to redefine their roles, and partly redefine the image they had of themselves. Our Munich manager actively made use of coaching and leadership and made good use of it. He handled the new situation very professionally and used it to his advantage. The Frankfurt manager was offered coaching as well, but didn't use it. He is still trying to grow into his newly defined role. The Berlin manager couldn't cope with the new situation. Due to the physical distance, he was at the headquarters infrequently, and subsequently had the least opportunity to play a part in the change itself. At the same time, people from the management board only visited these locations on rare occasions. It took them far too long to realize that there was a problem and getting on a plane for a visit. When the issue escalated, tension had already built up significantly over several months and escalated into a wave of resignations. In Berlin, six out of seven employees quit, practically shutting the site down. This could have been prevented with a vision for both the site and the people in charge. It also didn't help to let the branch office manager stay in the office after he had communicated that he was starting to look for a new job—yet another management failure.

After this setback, things started to improve. We are working on an overall branch office strategy. For new sites, at least local visions already exist. For example, we founded a branch office in Granada, Spain about a year ago. The strategy is to get well-educated people quicker on board than in Germany. Of course, these people cannot deliver consulting to German customers or provide training for them. They primarily support teams developing software for customers. This works quite well, because we thought about it carefully and accepted to invest the money saved in wages into traveling and technological equipment for remote working. The branch office is growing rapidly, confined only by the size and growth of the software projects developed by NovaTec teams. A vision is in place, management support is there, the branch office manager was included from the beginning and the business concept is working.

Sites within Germany now follow a different logic. Basically, there are two different types of branch offices we create: One is vowed to the center of life of our employees. The other one is a fully-fledged branch with new people, customers, and a business logic. If a couple of employees live at a place that makes traveling to headquarters every day difficult, we just rent office space where they live and call it a branch office. This is far better than having these people work from home 4 days a week, because then they don't have enough personal interaction with NovaTec colleagues and tend to slowly drift away until they finally quit. Providing an office near where they live brings people together and keeps a joint NovaTec spirit. While we probably could create a branch office for every single employee, this is not what we are aiming for. We look for teams. If there is no team, there won't be a branch office. This is also true for the second type of branch. We sometimes look for new investment opportunities and create a site for this reason. For example, Hannover (Germany) is attractive for us. There are many interesting companies that could potentially become our customers and there are enough universities around that could supply well-educated new employees. However, we still do not found a new branch office if none of our employees live near that location. Our way of thinking and our culture must be present there. This only happens if somebody has worked with us for several years and now wants to spend almost every day at the new office.

Of course, this multitude of new sites requires us to rise to the challenge of virtual working.

3.4 Virtual Working

The first rule of virtual working is: don't do it. The main reason is that colocated teams are on average about 40% more productive than dispersed (same team on different locations) or distributed (different teams on several locations) ones. A model that very neatly explains the reasons behind the drop in performance is called the "virtual distance model" (cf. Fig. 3.5), invented by Karen Sobel Lojeski and Richard R. Reilly (cf. Sobel & Reilly, 2008).

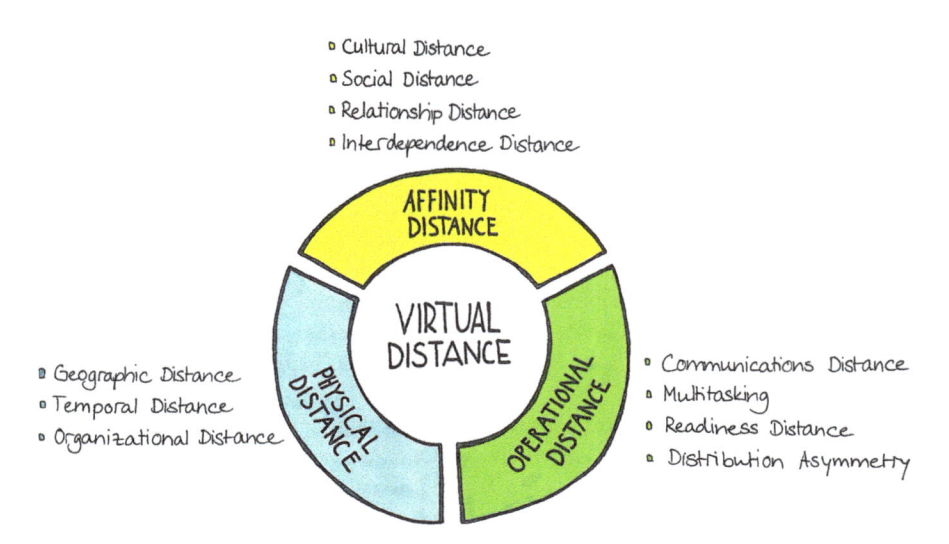

Fig. 3.5 The virtual distance model (cf. Sobel & Reilly, 2008, p. 48)

The authors state that virtual distance applies for every human interaction with another human being. It consists of three dimensions: Affinity distance, physical distance, and operational distance. While many other authors focus on "geographic distance," this model only sees it as a fraction of physical distance. It is supplemented by temporal distance and organizational distance.

Geographic distance means that people are physically apart—15 m or more. As soon as there are stairs involved, a wall, or too many steps to walk, you are faced with geographic distance (cf. Allen, 1984).

Temporal distance means that people are working asynchronously. This can either happen when people are working in different time-zones or simply when people start and end working at different times. For example, if somebody starts work at 7 and finishes at 3 while somebody else comes in at 11 and stays until 8 in the evening, you are faced with temporal distance.

Organizational distance basically means that there usually is a distance between different departments and organizations. You can spot this when people start talking about "us" and "them." Did you ever condemn "those marketing people"? Well, there you go...

As you can see, physical distance is far more complex than just "being in different countries."

This is similar with "operational distance," which basically means that the tools and framework conditions can pose a problem, contributing to virtual distance.

Communications distance is pretty obvious: You can convey less information via email than you can in a face-to-face conversation. Unfortunately, most people don't acknowledge this and communicate most of the day via email. I experienced many issues where just the communication channel used caused a major conflict in our team. All media can be considered according to its "media richness." The media mix must fit the needs of your team and environment. If it doesn't, you increase your operational distance.

Multitasking is also a bad thing, multiplying its effect in a virtual environment. Multitasking contributes to operational distance due to a lack in focus. People don't feel as close to one another if they are working on different things and they are continuously acting on edge due to the stress involved in task switching. Even if the stress level is low: If you have to choose which task to do first, you will usually work on the one for the people next to you, no matter how high its priority is, because your personal priority is made up of feeling close to somebody else.

Even if you heed those lessons, "readiness distance" can break your neck. It describes the "readiness" of your IT and communications infrastructure. Imagine that you have a beautiful communication strategy which involves video conferencing. Then you have your first meeting, switch on the equipment—and nothing happens. People grow inpatient while you try to fix it, call in your IT expert only to be told that "there is a license missing." Effects like not being able to hear the other person properly on the phone, having to enter complex pin numbers, or facing software updates just the moment you want to use the system are other examples of this type of distance.

Distribution Asymmetry is the last part of the puzzle to complete operational distance. It means an unbalanced distribution of your workforce. For example, if two of your people are working at the satellite site and five are in the group headquarters, you instantly get "them" and "us" again. This happens the other way around as well.

From my perspective, the most important distance category is the "affinity" distance. You can have it even if your people are sitting right next to each other. It comprises of cultural distance, social distance, relationship distance, and interdependence distance. You probably know cultural distance—it is created when people have different cultural backgrounds. This can be true within a country as well: In Germany, for example, there is a slightly different culture in "East" and "West" as well as between the different states. A Bavarian has a certain cultural distance when interacting with a "northern light" coming from Hamburg (any other state could have been chosen here as well).

Social distance means the status within society, that might oppose that of a team mate. Imagine an "Earl of Winchester," honored with a PhD and teaching at university, working together on a project, formally equal, with John Doe, who just has finished high school. Can you imagine any conflicts arising from that constellation? While this constructed example is quite obvious, there are many social nuances that have to be considered and addressed in a team if you want to keep the social distance low.

Relationship distance is described as "the extent to which you and others lack relationship connections from past work initiatives." Put simply: People don't know if they can trust each other, because they don't know their new colleagues. It manifests as a sense of unfamiliarity.

Interdependence distance happens mostly when there is no shared vision. People don't walk in the same direction and therefore don't commit to each other. Maybe you have spotted sentences like "well, my part is working, it's <put a name in> who has to fix his code, not me."

As you can see, there are many dimensions you have to consider when forming a virtual team (in addition to the "normal" issues to consider when forming any team, no matter if collocated or not). All of the aforementioned distances will occur, it's up to you to make them transparent and to address them. They are not bad in themselves—they are natural. It's easier of course, if you stay with colocated teams. It reduces your project complexity. Unfortunately, 65% of the teams in the IT industry are not colocated but distributed or dispersed. Those teams will be (on average) less productive than the colocated ones. But they can be of strategical importance and there usually are reasons why the companies go for them.

As described above, NovaTec has two reasons for using virtual teams: Having employees living far from headquarters and needing additional people not available in Germany. We are still working on overcoming the distance, but we already learned some valuable lessons I want to share with you. First, we will take a look at our team, then we will look beyond the borders and investigate other parts of NovaTec.

Our team has one iron rule: Be in the office on Fridays. Every Friday for everybody. Two out of three Fridays for people living far away. Rare exceptions are allowed for people if a week was particularly stressful. Having personal interaction with people is the only way to overcome virtual distance sustainably. Some time ago we focused more on customers and asked our team mates to also work on customer sites on Fridays. This very quickly led to people becoming alienated from each other, so we changed that again. Then we faced the issue of people working with internal stakeholders at NovaTec on Fridays, not spending time with our team. This had the same effect. Self-organization failed to solve the problem, because the urge to help others is very strong with everybody in our team. Therefore, I had to issue the rule that every Friday morning, up to lunch time, solely belongs to our team. People have clear boundaries when working together is a must, which led to an immediately noticeable surge in morale and team spirit. This is reinforced by having our desks in one single office. No doors, no walls, we can all see each other all of the time. This includes my desk, of course. Our satellite-colleagues from Munich and Frankfurt also have desks in our office, even though this means providing two desks for them at different locations. We despise shared desks, everybody has a fixed one. This creates a feeling of "coming home" when entering the room. Everybody knows where they belong and where to find each other. Also, this allows us to use the walls as information radiators. All kinds of information are displayed on our walls, from Delegation Board (cf. Management3.0f and Sect. 9.1) to contribution margins. Only half of this information is also represented in a digital tool (a wiki system), because it's simply unnecessary to duplicate more.

The resulting close relationship everybody enjoys enables us to use technology when not in the same room. For this purpose, we have high-quality hands-free conference devices that can be connected via Bluetooth to every phone or computer. They were not even expensive, but their ease of use is exceptional. For smaller meetings, we use a laptop with camera, connect the Jabra, stand around the table and chat while seeing and hearing everybody. For bigger meetings, we go into a meeting room equipped with a room camera and a bigger (as well as costlier) conference phone system. Unfortunately, we still do not have a remote presence robot available. Therefore, there is no physical interaction with remote people and we have to take pictures of work results and send them around. This is clumsy and not state of the art.

For slow or long asynchronous communication we use email. For quick and short asynchronous interaction, we use a group messenger app on our phones. This works quite well. It is interesting to see that people share private photos and information through this system as well—a good sign in terms of relatedness of the team members.

Another effort we undertake to decrease virtual distance is pair working. Whenever we get the chance we go to customers together and work there hand-in-hand. When somebody joins our team, we usually don't expect that person to earn money from the start. Instead, we send new colleagues out along with as many of our team members as possible to learn from them by engaging together at their customers. This also bonds people and reduces relationship distance.

The most important tool we use is called Sococo (sococo.com). While the application is suboptimal in terms of video quality, hole-punching and other important technology aspects, the developers really understand the concept of virtual distance. The most important features are a virtual office landscape and ease of use. Whenever we want to talk virtually, we just open Sococo, click on an empty room (usually our competence area room) and the connection is established without any further action required. In terms of reducing readiness distance, this is the best concept we have seen so far.

The tools and technologies mentioned are used all over the company at NovaTec. The concept of bringing people together often to bridge relatedness gaps is used to different extents. Some competence areas only bring their people together once each quarter. These same people complain about not feeling like a team and experiencing low performance. Other competence areas follow the same approach as lived by us. Interestingly, when starting our Granada branch office, we very clearly expressed that we wanted our people to travel there and our Spanish colleagues to fly in to us as often as possible. Saving money is not a primary goal with this site. This was and is our key concept for making nearshoring successful. This is the key rule to decrease virtual distance.

3.5 Learnings

You definitely should analyze and consider changing your current organizational structure. In our case, we consequently asked our people what aspects were helpful and which were not. We listened and acted on the feedback. Within our business unit of agile methods, we flattened hierarchies and let incompatible employees go. The basic idea in our CA is to have cross-functional teams without specific areas of expertise that are confident enough to talk directly to everybody and to ignore hierarchies whenever needed. The stance of the boss must be one of being at eye to eye level with the team, not overestimating his self-importance. One of our main mantras is: "Don't ask for permission, ask for forgiveness." However, in our case there are still situations where as the boss I have to decide things the team doesn't want to, even though they should be able to handle it themselves.

We also learned that a structure must fit the type of employees you have. If you change the structure, this might also change the type of employee you are looking for, also leading to people leaving your organization.

When looking at the bigger picture, we also changed a lot there. We achieved more clarity by removing our department heads, moving their duties to the competence area managers, who actually work with the people they are responsible for. It is not a good idea to make somebody accountable for something they have no idea of, for example when bosses don't see their employees at work. To increase the CA managers ability to fulfill their duties, we allowed them to delegate most aspects to the whole team, or to individuals. Titles are no longer the prerequisite for gaining responsibility.

With the CA managers in charge, we morphed the former organizational buckets into autonomous value-creation units. Competence areas are now accountable for their own profitability and their overall contribution to NovaTec. Of course, they can only do this while being allowed to hire and fire their own employees and to create their own strategies.

These autonomous value-units are not dependent on each other, there is no "hierarchy of departments." However, there are some support functions that are still dominant and considered "must-use" in the organization. They already started to change as well and will continue to do so, otherwise they face the risk of "dying" because the competence areas choose to satisfy their needs without them. This is also true for the senior management function, because the value-units are able to ignore management, which is the equivalent of letting them "die." Of course, this works the other way as well: If a competence area does not produce the value expected, it will be shut down, which we already did several times. In doing this, we learned some valuable lessons and are now better at failing, which is a very important skill in the agile world.

Some of our biggest mistakes revolve around leaving people out of the loop with important decisions or not providing coaching and leadership for them to deal with the change affecting them.

Satellite sites are especially prone for having trouble with change, especially when left out of the decision process. We realized that you need a vision for both the site and the people in charge. If a key player announces that he will not support the change and would prefer to leave, release that person from work immediately. This is true for all kinds of satellite sites, be it nearshoring, center-of-life, or market penetration offices.

With nearshoring, we are not trying to save money. The primary reason is to attract talent we cannot attract in Germany. From my point of view, this is the primary reason for our Granada office to be successful. Before that we failed in Jeddah, because we didn't have a solid concept in place. It might sound trivial, but carefully think about your vision, strategy, management support, technological equipment, travel opportunities, and cost structure before opening a new site.

With these structural changes in place we are noticing a steep increase in employee happiness and other metrics. We do believe that changing the organizational structure nourished the soil for growing teams, establishing trust, and making better decisions.

Unaffected by the provisions mentioned above is our need for virtual working. I strongly believe that you should avoid this kind of setup if you can, because you always have to struggle with virtual distance, which leads to diminished productivity. We accepted this fundamental truth and tried to minimize virtual distance with a couple of arrangements. The most important one is that we force our team to work together physically every week, with rare exceptions. We also created a work environment where people feel welcome, which means everybody has their own fixed desk in our team room at headquarters, no matter how often she is in this office. This is supplemented by good technological infrastructure, focusing on ease-of-use rather than highest technical standards. Especially virtual rooms with zero-click-conferencing capabilities help us a lot. A messenger app allows for asynchronous communication without the need to start a computer. The only devices missing are virtual presence robots, but they are on the wish-list. However, as mentioned above, the primary rule we learned with virtual working is to meet in person. This means a lot of traveling for everybody, but cannot be avoided if you want to create teams and keep them healthy.

Changing Leadership

When changing an organizational culture, which is the case when transitioning to agile, leadership must change as well. This is valid for both the people filling leadership positions and the style of leadership applied. Both are difficult. In our case this essentially means a major shift from command-and-control thinking toward self-organization. It feels more like a journey than an end-state for us, but I nevertheless strongly believe that this is the future of leadership.

4.1 Leadership and Management Tasks

Before we take a closer look at the leadership style we are aiming for, or the people filling leadership positions, we should investigate the tasks associated with this phrase. For us, leadership is what somebody does that leads to you wanting to follow the ideas of this person. Leadership is inspirational and motivating. It is about crafting visions, creating innovations, and caring about people.

Management, on the other hand, is what somebody does to help you follow a vision. It is about providing structure and rules. Management coordinates people, plans and organizes stuff. It is about caring for processes.

Not every manager is a leader, but in my opinion, every leader must also be able to manage. However, good leaders usually don't want to manage much, which plays on the idea of self-organizing teams. With agile, the same amount of management tasks must be done as in a traditional enterprise. The difference is that with agile, it is many people getting the job done while in the traditional enterprise it usually is a small caste of managers working on it.

At NovaTec we distributed many tasks to several roles. It usually is a combination of leadership and management duties. The most important roles for us are the management board, competence area managers, competence group leaders, career coaches, branch office managers, and team members.

The management board is ultimately accountable for the success or failure of the enterprise. While they delegate most of the work, they have to fulfill some major responsibilities. First, they must create and provide an overarching vision and strategy for the whole enterprise. While they don't have to define every single aspect themselves, they have to make sure the strategy meets their expectations. This is also valid for founding new branch offices, be it in Germany or abroad. New satellite sites have to match the strategy. The management board also must decide which new competence areas or service departments (e.g., HR) should be set up, and which ones should be discontinued. One major responsibility in doing this is to find the right people to lead such endeavors. Competence area managers, (service) department heads, and satellite site managers must be carefully chosen in order for the overall vision to come to life. Also, in everything we do, the board must make sure the legal requirements, such as bookkeeping, are met.

These tasks are not new for a management board in general. For us they were. Everything that had to do with leadership had been conducted by the old CEO in phase one. The other board members were tending to management tasks or even regular work. People management, like leading and managing competence area managers or department heads, was not in place back then. Focusing on these types of tasks now is a change for the board members, today consisting of four people. There are still cases where board members are doing regular team tasks like creating reports or writing sales offers. The people doing so are well equipped for it and the result is good, but the leadership tasks mentioned above don't get done. This is the main reason why we still need four board members and seven competence area managers for 200 employees.

The competence area managers support the management board by providing five areas of services to their business units (cf. Fig. 3.3): Strategy and area content, profitability, personal development, disciplinary management, and motivation.

The first responsibility contains the definition and application of vision and strategy for the specific competence area. Business models must be crafted, enticing visions to come to life, specifying the topics a competence area deals with, as well as the topics an area does not deal with. For example, we defined that software testing and test strategies are not part of the competence are of "agile methods," because it derails our focus on organizational change and dives too deeply into the technical domain.

Of course, these business models must be profitable. For us this means earning money with consulting and training services, both individually and as a team, in every project. Usually, every employee should create more revenue than costs. However, with some topics or people we deviate from this rule. For example, if the topic is new or the consultant didn't earn herself a name yet, it is okay to stay unprofitable for some time. The competence area manager makes sure the right people are on the right projects for the right price, and also takes care to assemble the right mix of skills in the team.

The key to increased profitability in our profession is skill. The better somebody is at what they do, the easier it is to sell that person's services to a customer and to realize a higher price. Therefore, personal development is of utmost importance. We institutionalized quarterly development dialogues (more often, if the employee wants it), created a development concept, illustrating what to do in order to reach a particular skill level, and put a mentoring concept in place so every employee has somebody more skilled available for support every day. We definitely want our employees to grow quickly. To further support this, we created the role of "career coach." The competence area manager can delegate the development dialogues to this role, as long as the coachee agrees to this. The goal is to achieve excellence in one or more topics the competence area deals with.

Once a certain skill level is achieved, team members can create new content and assets to increase the value the team can deliver to our customers. It is expected from the competence area manager to either embody excellence in the area topics and lead through example, or to make sure somebody else in the competence area radiates subject matter brilliance. If this task is delegated, a competence group leader is created, with disciplinary leadership maintained by the competence area manager.

Disciplinary management contains, in our case, performance appraisals, promotions, salary raises, disciplinary and legal actions. It is up to the competence area manager how to deal with these topics. We are trying to handle them in an agile a way as possible, you can read more about them in Chap. 9. In phase one, all of this was done by board members. Today, they are only involved in very special cases, usually as advisors rather than decision-makers. This was probably our biggest step in empowering people.

Motivation is the fluffiest responsibility a competence area manager has. I strongly believe that you cannot motivate people intrinsically, and extrinsic motivators like money are of limited use. You can demotivate them by providing the wrong processes and conditions, but if an employee doesn't feel motivated to work, you cannot change that. Not even with bribes or violence—these extrinsic motivators might get the employee to do the job, but they won't get him intrinsically motivated. It is intrinsic motivation we are looking for. To support this, we try to create a system through and around our employees that allows them to fulfill their motivational needs. The system largely consists of:

- Finding out who is motivated by what (cf. Sect. 2.2)
- Providing a real team environment
- Providing recognition often
- Allowing everybody to learn and increase their skills
- Providing meaning by having clear goals within the competence areas and projects
- Allowing employees to bring their own ideas to life
- Making sure everybody gets the projects they want and match

You already read about creating teams in Chap. 2. That chapter also explained how we provide recognition through Kudo Cards. In addition, as the manager I try to praise employees as often and as appropriately and possible. On special occasions, I can use a special "pizza budget" to reward the team. It is important not to use this budget for individual rewards, because that would negatively influence our team dynamics.

You can learn more about skills and development in Chap. 8 and goals are investigated in Chap. 6. One main example of how we allow employees to bring their own ideas to life can be found in Sect. 9.2. Generally, every employee can raise any idea with either her competence area manager or with the management board. If it is well thought-out, we implement it. In our business unit, we conduct monthly retrospective sessions and whenever a good idea is raised, we follow up on it.

Making sure everybody gets the projects they want and match is the most difficult task concerning motivation. Many factors must be considered, for example travel preferences of the employee, expected marginal return, overall and business unit profit impact, project importance, attractiveness of the project content, existing and required competence level, opportunities for personal growth, and many more. This area is the one where self-organization fails most often for us. Some team members prefer not to think too far ahead or decline projects without considering all relevant parameters. Therefore, I as the competence area manager have to micromanage quite often, even though I would love to not lift a single finger for this kind of task.

As you can see, the management board addressed the shortfall in leadership and management across the organization by enriching the competence area manager role. This role is overburdened though and people filling it need to delegate some of the tasks as well. Competence group leaders, career coaches, and the teams are the primary delegates.

The competence group leader role changed massively in phase three. Back in phase one, I experienced it as a meaningless title with the obligation to do performance appraisals if the competence area manager didn't want to do them himself. Today, competence group leaders are true experts in at least some of the topics the competence area does business in. They show this kind of excellence to the outside world, are present at conferences, and write articles. If the competence area manager prefers to focus on management tasks, competence group leaders inherit the technical leadership tasks within the area, whereby "technical" stands for anything the competence area does business with. If the business unit covers a wide area of topics, there might be several competence groups, each one clustering a specific set of services and knowledge. In the case of "agile methods," we did not install competence group leaders yet, because I want to lead technically and prefer to delegate management tasks. In addition, the size of our competence area didn't force us to think about scaling, yet. So, for me, competence group leaders do not yet relieve me of work. Career coaches do.

Career coaches engage in development dialogues with employees. They are trained in professional coaching (as are the competence area managers) and are able to assume a coaching stance whenever useful. Each competence area selects their career coaches by asking for volunteers, then training them for and on the job. Two experienced coaches from my team teach, mentor and coach the other career coaches in the organization. We also institutionalized a "career coach community" to learn from each other and to streamline some basic processes. Employees can now volunteer to have their dialogues either with their competence area manager or with one of the career coaches. These talks happen as often as the coachee wants, but at least once each quarter. The topics are chosen by the coachee while the methods are chosen by the coach. This means the responsibility for individual development resides with the coachee, not with the coach or the manager. If the coachee chooses to talk about advancing in rank or how to earn more money, this is what the development dialogue will be about. If the coachee asks for a discussion on a specific project situation, this is what the coaching session will deal with.

The career coaches formally have no right to decide anything, unless explicitly granted by the competence area manager. Their skills are their power. They can help their coachees to see new opportunities and to learn more about themselves. The good thing about this is that they never have a hidden agenda, as is sometimes the case with competence area managers. The coaches are able to fully focus on their coachees and fully assume their perspective.

Personally, I greatly appreciate this role. Everybody involved profits from it. However, I insist on every new team member to do their development dialogues with me for the first 6 months. This allows me to get to know the person and to see how quickly she acts on her own wishes. It also allows me to recognize problems early and—in the worst case—to dismiss the person within the first 6 months of employment (in Germany it is very difficult to do that after this timespan).

Career coaches are regular team members with special skills. These skills make them eligible as career coaches. They don't hold any higher rank or title however. They just have the aptitude and desire to coach other people. Many other tasks can also be delegated to the team. Some work better than others, of course. You can read more about our approach in Sect. 9.1.

We should also not forget about the branch office managers. They are NovaTec's face to the public at our satellite sites. Depending on the person and location, this role is shaped differently, which mainly means the number of days (50–90%) we expect these managers to earn money in customer projects. Their main duty is to care for the people working at their branch office, acquire new regional customers, and find new talent for us. Of course, they also take care of enabling management tasks like renting office space, equipping them with furniture, and scouting for training locations.

4.2 Leadership Style

Our management and leadership tasks are numerous, which is normal in all organizations across the globe. What is not so obvious is the style we try to apply on these tasks. Basically, we try to do as little command-and-control and as much self-organization as possible. The reason for this is our basic belief that we live and work in a complex domain. "Complex" is a specific phrase in the agile domain, most often explained with models such as the "Stacey Chart" (cf. Fig. 4.1).

While this model is no longer promoted by the original author, Ralph Stacey, it still serves its purpose as a facilitation tool for discussion. Try to picture it as three-dimensional. The first dimension is "requirements," standing for "what" has to be done. "Technology" describes "how" these things will be done. The third dimension is called "people" and signifies "who" will do it. All axes have the same meaning.

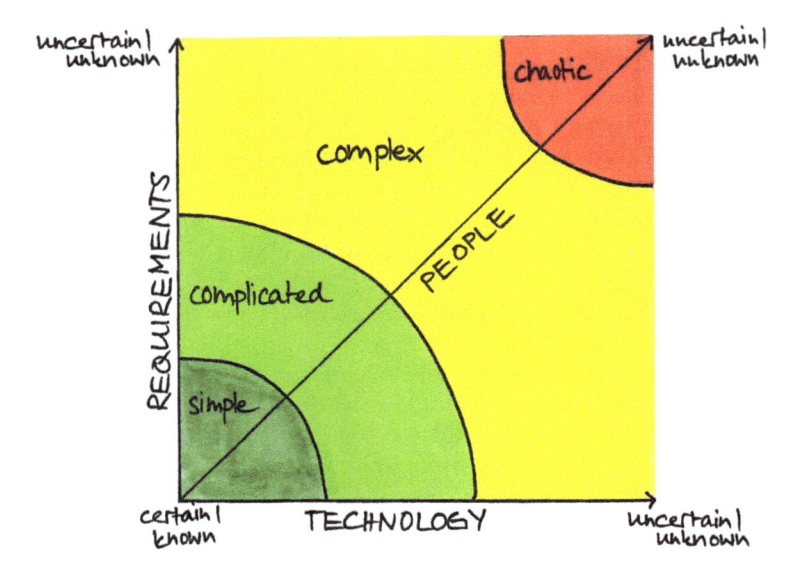

Fig. 4.1 Complexity domains, Based on Stacey (1996, p. 47) and Schwaber and Beedle (2002, p. 93)

The lower left corner means, that a specific dimension is absolutely clear and won't change in the future. The outer ends of each axis mean that nothing is clear and many changes must be expected. Within this system, there are four areas (try to picture them as spheres in a three-dimensional world), expressing specific domains. "Simple" is described as everything is certain. "Complicated" means more is known than unknown. In the "complex" domain more is unknown than known and if you face a "chaotic" environment, basically nothing is certain.

George Box coined the aphorism: "All models are wrong, but some are useful." This is true for the model above as well. However, when talking about living in a complex world, I want to express that more is unknown than known. In our business, we don't know what the customer will need in a year from now—and in some cases even tomorrow—as their environment is changing very rapidly. Usually, we also don't know what technology, methods, or other tools will deliver this benefit to the customer. And most certainly, our team members are normal human beings, showing all kinds of social interactions, conflicts, and unexpected behavior as much as anybody else. To address complexity, you must use appropriate tools and micromanagement certainly doesn't get you far. In addition, it is not desired by today's employees, especially the younger ones.

This is actually interesting to observe, because these younger employees are the ones shouting for self-organization the loudest, while needing the largest amount of micromanagement at the same time. It is a very exciting dance to bring both needs together and to develop the whole team to a full autonomy, both individually and as a unit. Situational leadership is the basic requirement for this. While the goal in everything we do is full empowerment, sometimes our skills aren't well developed

4.2 Leadership Style

enough to achieve it. In these cases, we have to rely on different leadership styles. For me as a leader the distinction is sometimes difficult, causing me to use an imperfect approach every now and then. Luckily, we live a very open feedback culture, providing me with instant feedback. For example, one of my team members wrote three sticky notes with the words "management 1.0," "2.0," and "3.0" (cf. Sect. 1.2) on them. Whenever he catches me relying on a traditional style of command-and-control management, he raises the "1.0" card to remind me of our goals.

The term most often used in literature describing an agile leadership style is "servant leadership." The basic idea is for the manager to serve her employees by providing a great environment to thrive in and by moving blockers out of the way while leaving everything else to the team. Personally, I no longer believe that this is the right thing to do in every situation. I agree on this as a vision and additionally believe that a certain maturity in employees must be present for it to work out. If this level of maturity is not present, servant leadership can only be part of the story, needing additional leadership styles for people with lower maturity. My personal experience is that about 10% of employees are at this stage to start with and 40 more percent can be developed up to this maturity level. I did not succeed with the other 50% so far—ask me again in a couple of years.

Increasing the maturity level needs a lot of work. Our approach is described throughout this book, all of it plays its part. However, I want to highlight some especially important aspects: trust, transparency, and delegation.

When you learn something new, you will make mistakes. When I went to an archery range with my team, I wasn't even able to hit the giant rubber Grizzly. Three arrows, no hit, triple frustration. But that was fine. Nobody expected me to excel the first time. Think back to things you did for the first time and then apply your experience on your team. Working in a self-organized manner is new for most of them. They aren't good at it, yet. They will make mistakes. Your job now is to prevent lethal errors (like me shooting one of my team members instead of the rubber Grizzly) by designing a system that prevents just that (people have to stand behind the archer), ideally by means of mentoring and coaching. Other than that, trust your employees to give their best and to act upon their learnings. Only if there is no action following mistakes should you start to worry.

For this level of trust to work, a high level of transparency is needed, both for you and your employees. Only when your team knows what you expect of them and you know what they are actually doing, can you let go of control. In our case, conflicts only arise when transparency failed. For example, we struggle over and over again with professional behavior toward colleagues in other business units and customers. It took a while until we realized that the source of this behavior were different definitions of the term "professionalism." While we all agreed on professionalism as both a core and wish value, each and every one of us understood it differently. Once we identified this dysfunction, we at least knew where the problems were coming from and could start working on them. It's still not fully solved though, because mental models aren't easy to change.

The third main pillar of advancing the maturity level of your employees is delegation. The more you ask your team instead of making the decision yourself (cf. Sect. 9.1), the higher the need for the team members to assume a stance of responsibility. If you do this often enough, and respect the team's decision, you will be able to witness a gradual increase in self-organization. Unfortunately, this only goes up to a certain point. There seems to be a barrier for some people to make the mental jump from "I can make this decision" to "I am accountable for this decision." My plan for the next couple of years is to find out if these colleagues just need a little bit longer than others to make this step, if they are not willing to try, or if this is a personal trait, meaning some people might just not be able to do this.

This leadership style is particularly challenging because it pushes everybody out of their comfort zones. More is demanded of the team members than usual, they don't have a father figure that does the thinking for them. More is also demanded from the leaders, because they need to work on the system instead of micromanaging, which is far more difficult than just assigning today's work to today's available resources. This constant strain needs special people. However, once you achieved a certain level of self-organization, working life is more fulfilling and self-directed than before, which makes up for the initial efforts.

4.3 People Filling Leadership Positions

Are you a leader? How do you know? I believe that skill beats title. Many organizations in Germany and across the world, including NovaTec, attach great importance to titles. Do you hire people who have not attended university? If you do, do you pay them the same as the ones who have? Logically, if somebody has studied a topic at university, they have typically invested around 80 h into the seminar. Working on it in a business context only takes you 2 weeks (40 h per week) to reach the same level. I admit that having studied 4 years at university proves a point, but for me this doesn't mean somebody who hasn't is worth less (literally). At NovaTec, we still look primarily for people with university degrees and emphasize titles. While this might make sense for some positions, it is not helpful for leaders. Leadership aptitude can only be learned in real life, not in university classes. Still, my own business card has four titles on it: My two university degrees, my consultant level, and my position as competence area manager. This is ridiculous. In phase one, there was no way around it. I tried to change it back then, but was rebuked by the CEO. Today, nobody has tried to change it again (the scars run deep), but we have it on the backlog for our team. Our customers want to know what skill we possess. This does not necessarily require someone to know how many years we spent at university. Especially in times of social networking, we don't need all the details on the card, but just the essentials.

This is my basic philosophy for leaders: Skill beats title. Everybody can be a leader, if they have the skill and mindset. Missing skills can be learned, however a certain mindset is difficult to change. That means you have to choose people with the right mindset rather than ones with the right history of certifications and qualifications. What I am looking for in leaders is a can-do attitude, people who are looking for solutions rather than making themselves and everyone else miserable by just seeing problems. In addition, I am looking for leaders who want to empower people, rather than believing they are the smartest person in the room. A leader needs to want to see the best of his employees instead of wanting them to see the best in himself. Also, you should train your leaders in coaching and mentoring, which means that they must want to learn these skills. This leads to the most important trait of a leader: the inherent motivation for continuous improvement. If someone hasn't read a single book about leadership or management within the last 6 months, he shouldn't be in a leadership or management position!

Should you realize that some of the people filling important positions don't exhibit these traits, remove them quickly. You cannot allow bad examples to lead, because they are the living role model to all of your employees. What they do will be what your staff mirrors. If they mess up, many others will as well. You can't allow that. That's the main reason why we exchanged all department heads at the end of phase two.

A really bad example at NovaTec was the struggle with the former CEO in phase two. After it had become apparent that it wouldn't work out to win him over for a new management style, it took more than 2 years to remove him. While it is honorable that everything was done to help him change his stance and to adapt to the new requirements, in my opinion it was obvious much earlier that he wouldn't adjust. The paralysis of the enterprise could have been removed at least a year earlier. It is difficult to know for sure, but I am quite certain we would have lost fewer people this way.

4.4 Learnings

To create an agile environment, it is absolutely necessary to shift from a command-and-control style of management to self-organization and leadership. "Changing management" applies to both the management style and the people doing the job. This is very difficult and not everybody will be able or willing to live up to the task.

At NovaTec, we defined many different management and leadership tasks. Some of them (local sales, customer acquisition, on-site leadership and branch office management) are delegated from the management board to the site manager and others are delegated to the competence area managers. The competence area managers can delegate them to somebody else as well. The main areas of responsibility for competence area managers are strategy and area content, profitability, personal development, disciplinary management, and motivation. We defined competence group leaders as the primary delegate for content-related tasks, career coaches for personal development. Most remaining activities can be delegated within the teams, especially if we apply a Delegation Board approach for clarity. Only disciplinary tasks remain with the competence area managers and cannot be delegated.

These tasks need to be worked by exhibiting an agile leadership style. We believe that we live and work in the complex domain, meaning more is unknown than known. Therefore, we cannot rely on the skill of a single manager but rather need to dip into the knowledge and power of every team member. In addition, this is expected by many employees, especially younger ones. Unfortunately, not everybody already possesses the skill of good self-organization, which means the manager needs to apply different methods situationally and trust employees, accepting that not everything will work out right first time. It means asking instead of deciding and creating an environment of trust and transparency. It also means taking the stance of a "servant" to the team instead of assuming they exist to "serve" the manager's bidding. This agile way of management is very demanding and will definitely push everybody involved out of their comfort zones.

Since this is not only rewarding but also very demanding, people filling leadership positions need to be carefully selected. Skill beats title, so in my opinion, everybody could be a leader. Choose people with the right mindset, missing skills can be learned. For me, the major aspects of an agile leader's mindset are: a can-do attitude, looking for solutions instead of problems, empowering people, not believing they are the smartest person in the room, wanting to see the best of their employees, and striving for continuous improvement. The last aspect is the most important one—without a strong drive for continuous improvement, nobody can succeed in such an environment. If somebody shows the wrong attitude, educate them. If this produces no change, remove them from leadership positions. Your leaders are multipliers for everybody in the organization, so don't allow them to show the wrong attitude.

Changing Focus

As you could see in the last chapter, we focus quite intensely on specific traits in our leaders. Focus is extremely important, not only in Scrum where it is one of the core values, but also in every organization on the planet. Missing focus means spreading limited resources (like money or the time of your employees) too thinly across many things, resulting in doing nothing really well. Focus is a universal ingredient to success. It can be applied on many different levels and aspects. The following chapters will shine a light on how we shifted the focus of our organization and the one of our managers. Then, we will dive into one specific and very important thing we focus on: employee happiness.

5.1 Focus of the Organization

Every organization should have a focus. Usually, it is described as a vision, combined with a strategy. Ideally, this focus is acted upon, meaning what's written down is actually what people do inside the organization. Many organizations don't value focus very much and "diversify" in a way that doesn't make sense. NovaTec was one of them.

Back in phase one there was no notable focus at all. There was no vision and no strategy. Basically, we pursued whatever idea somebody had, as long as this person was important enough to us. For example, when our CEO wanted to establish a branch office in Saudi Arabia, we did that even though we didn't have a business concept, customers or employees there. In addition, our portfolio was largely unmanaged. We didn't know our own products and services across the organization and still invested more money in additional ideas. Back then, we were in the consulting business, as well as body leasing (renting employees to customers), software development for customers, creating and selling our own software products, and reselling software products of other companies. All different types of products with differing markets, needing different types of management. We at least managed them all consistently, that was with an equal non-existent amount of

Fig. 5.1 Phase one focus

attention. Imagine a 100 small boats going in different directions if you want to visualize the situation in phase one (cf. Fig. 5.1).

To maintain at least some sort of profitable operation, our management decided to use a KPI for the lucrative parts of NovaTec's business. It was the hours every single employee worked at the customer's site. We didn't have any information systems available back then, so we didn't know about contribution margins or other meaningful metrics. Accepting this fact and coming up with a measure of hours worked was certainly better than doing nothing. Unfortunately, this didn't help in choosing the right projects from a financial point of view. Instead, we accepted pretty much every project coming around the corner as long as we were able to staff it. All this resulted in very poor performance of the enterprise. Even though our consulting results were good, we invested all the money back into bad ideas in phase one and still carry the burden of a bad customer distribution, posing a certain risk for us.

This started to change in phase three. Even though we are still working on a well-formulated strategy, we actually already act as if it was in place. During phase two, several competence areas created their own visions and strategies, largely unnoticed by the still struggling management board. On top of that, the competence area managers, together with the management board, installed a couple of rules to coordinate the work of the organization as such. These strategies and rules are still in place and allow us to act in a coordinated fashion.

As you read in Sect. 3.3, we decided on key aspects of when to create or close a branch office. Most of them are located in Germany, because certain regions in Germany are defined as our focus of business activity. Within these regional areas, we offer a defined portfolio of services and largely abandoned software products if they don't support our consulting work. Actually, we made most of them open source. Only a single NovaTec software is still sold and considered a standalone product. Decisions about portfolio changes are made very consciously, based on facts rather than dreams.

Fig. 5.2 2017 focus

We also abandoned the success criterion of "hours worked at customers," because it is meaningless without additional information. We are focusing on contribution margins instead, usually clustered at team level. Since teams exist both on projects and in competence areas, we are able to see if a service, product area, or customer project is lucrative for us, which in turn allows us to choose projects more sensibly. In 2017 we even took it further and decided on financial goals on competence area level, based on monthly numbers, for the very first time. We even communicated them to everybody. For us, this is new and huge!

The situation today can be pictured as a 100 little boats, going almost into the same direction, and always moving in clusters that are closely aligned inside (cf. Fig. 5.2).

In addition to this huge change, the organization—while never forgetting our customers' needs—shifted its overall focus very much toward the employees, starting with leadership and the right people filling these positions. We are still working on it, but already see some success in what we do. For example, we were substantially more profitable in 2017 than back in phases one and two.

We are far from being perfect, but the enterprise is taking form slowly. The next goals are to finalize our strategy and add a broader industry focus to it.

5.2 Focus of Managers

Choosing the right people to fill management and leadership positions is not enough. These managers also have to develop a common focus. In phase one, responsibilities were unclear and nobody actually cared about it. Thus, it was coincidence if the right or the wrong people were put into power. In effect, every manager focused on something else. For most of them this meant spending as much time as possible on their own customer projects. Some of them defined success as earning more money than anybody else, both for the company and for themselves. Hardly anybody focused on developing our common business or improving the environment at NovaTec. Unfortunately, even if they would have chosen to do so, there were no information systems available to allow them to make fact-based decisions. It's a funny twist in the course of events that our competence area of "agile methods" was the one to implement information systems first, even though agilists are usually not fond of processes or information systems. We had to do it however, as we needed to know what was working and what wasn't. We were a young business unit with a desperate need for information to take the right decisions and become profitable. Only 2 years after we used them to our benefit, the rest of the organization adopted the idea and ditched our prototypes in favor of more sophisticated systems. The reason for this long reaction time is that before phase three, the management board did not show any sign of focus. In phase one, this in my opinion was due to the omnipotent CEO, while in phase two everybody was focusing on the internal struggle, leaving no energy for other ideas. The misunderstanding was also present that this kind of transparency was an enemy, rather than a powerful ally.

Today in phase three, the focus of management is noticeable and shifting. One could say that the management board is focusing on removing the lack of focus we had when phase three started. This impacts many areas, one of which is the availability of information systems. We realized that we need numbers to manage, and spreadsheets are not enough. The first focus of every manager in the organization today is the KPI of contribution margins. They are relevant for us both on team and individual levels. The hours worked are still a number of interest for most managers, but they are secondary to the contribution margins and backed by real data pulled from our systems.

All this information is used to support the three major focus areas of every manager at NovaTec: business area development, skill development, and employee happiness. These focus areas are strongly correlated and influence each other. Focusing on the business area development automatically means increasing the skill level of oneself and all employees, which usually results in happier employees. At the same time, people who are happy improve results disproportionately, learn faster, and stay with the company longer.

It is great that our managers have focus today. Some things are still not great in terms of management's focus though. For example, we are starting too many different initiatives at once, leading to finishing them far more slowly than would otherwise be possible. We are not reaching flow on management level, but are struggling with an overflowing queue. Part of this is due to the fact that our management board is focusing not only on board tasks, but also on many operative activities. This is inefficient on a strategic level. Our information systems are just now slowly starting to show this fact, because they are still not state-of-the-art. They are improving every month, and I am sure that we will reach a decent level within the next year. This might help us to solve another issue of unfocused action, which is the coordination between the different competence areas. Right now, every CA focuses on different industries, customers, strategies, etc. While this was necessary in phase two, it should be aligned somewhat more closely today.

In all of this, our biggest risk is to fall back into old habits. This could far too easily happen. Delegating work you like is difficult, as is focusing on something you are not yet an expert in. For example, we started to measure happiness (cf. Sects. 5.3 and 6.2). I led this initiative with great vigor and had to learn to pass it on to somebody else once it was a common practice. This was difficult for me, but I succeeded after a while and passed it to our HR department. We still have to wait and see how this will work out.

5.3 Happiness

Employee happiness is our secret sauce. If you try to adopt anything from this book, make this your focus area. It is our belief that trying to keep people happy is the right thing to do. If this doesn't persuade you, keep in mind that happiness is immensely important, because it is expensive to find new employees and happy employees are loyal employees. Also, work results seem to be better with happy workers. The topic is so important to us that our competence area's vision reads: "Together, discovering and creating a happier way of working."

For us this means that, as a team, we want to be happy and help others find happiness in what they do. This holds especially true for our customers. If there is no obvious way visible at the moment, we will work to discover one. This stance was adopted by the overall organization. We started measuring happiness across the organization, which is described from a metrics point of view in Sect. 6.2. Here, we will focus on the topic itself.

In phase one, there was only one employee survey a year, asking a million questions, with hardly anybody acting on the results. Today we ask a simple question every quarter and actually derive actions from it. The question is a net promoter score (NPS), asking "How likely is it that you would recommend NovaTec to your friends?" on a ten-point scale. Below the online question is an open text field, simply asking: "Why did you choose this number?"

From this open response, we derive what issues to tackle next. If we realize a pattern we usually set up another survey specifically asking for this aspect, gathering more information and devising an action plan if the problem appears to be widespread. As long as the management board acts on the feedback, employees feel listened to and valued. As soon as management stops acting, this will be reflected in rapidly declining happiness scores.

Another reflection of our happiness focus can be found in our employee-led improvement system. We called it "SMILE" (no acronym, it just seemed to fit the purpose). The goal is to improve issues the employees care about. Every employee who wants to lead or support this endeavor is welcome to join, there is no elitist selection process, and there is no manager on the SMILE committee.

Any employee can suggest as many ideas as they want, by just entering a ticket into a simple ticketing system, set up for this purpose. Employees enter the benefit and the costs of their idea, assisted by a member of the SMILE team. Once an idea is sufficiently well spelled out, it can be voted on by all employees. At all times, all tickets are publicly accessible to everybody in the company. Every quarter, the top-voted ideas are implemented by the SMILE team. For this purpose, the management board provides a yearly budget (50.000 Euro in 2017). Ideas implemented so far range from better coffee beans to table football, a comfortable lounge area through to more work-related things such as height-adjustable desks or better mice and keyboards. If an idea is out of scope for SMILE, for example a change to central processes or ideas related to monetary compensation, it is highlighted to the management board. Management then decides what to do and either implements a change within the next quarter or explains to the employees why the current way of operating will remain as is. This is highly appreciated by the employees and results in higher happiness. It also means that management has two unusual feedback cycles with a broad community, namely the quarterly NPS surveys and SMILE. They don't have to come with their own ideas on what to improve next, they can just pick and choose from what people tell them about their observed needs. Very convenient.

Additionally, we created the role of feel-good manager. His job is, apart from working in customer projects for 50% of his time, to come up with even more ideas of how to improve happiness at the workplace. Everything that escapes the attention of management or people don't want to highlight in a survey or SMILE is brought forward by him. For some ideas, he is also responsible for implementing them, which is a relief for management who just have to make the decision and then pass it on to the feel-good manager. Some examples include: setting up a Spanish course to improve communications with Granada, organizing events (e.g., a yearly skiing event), organizing food trucks, improving processes such as new employee onboarding, etc.

As you can see, the whole happiness system is based on the principle of collecting ideas from all employees, prepare change suggestions for management and making sure the management board actually acts upon these suggestions. If one of these steps fails, happiness is likely to drop rapidly. Now that people know what a happier way of working can look like, they are very likely to miss a focus on happiness even more than if they had never known about it. There lies a huge risk in this simple truth. Should management stop to act and deliver on the demands, people will complain quickly and lose trust a little later. Due to the still imperfect focus of our board, this could happen if nobody pushes them to act and prepares suggestions. The systems are there, the question is if the people responsible for them will continue to take focused action.

5.4 Learnings

Focus is extremely important. Not only for us, but for every organization. Missing focus means spreading limited time and other resources thinly across many things and doing nothing well. Focus is relevant on all levels, be it the overall organization, managers, or workers. In my opinion, focus is a universal ingredient to success and focusing on employee happiness is our secret sauce.

5.4 Learnings

To apply focus, you need to start with vision and strategy. If there is no adequate one available, create your own for the context you are responsible for. Then tune your processes and information systems to it so they play well together. Try to draw (literally or mentally) an image of your organization's focus: Are there a 100 boats going into different directions, are there clusters moving jointly forward, or are all boats already sailing toward the same goal? For us, the biggest changes were in refocusing our portfolio, narrowing down the target market and moving away from hours worked to contribution margins. This only works with the right people filling management and leadership positions.

These managers have to focus themselves as well. Their role is more than just spending time at customers, it is about shaping the organization. If management doesn't show focus, the rest of the organization won't either. Some key areas for management focus are meaningful metrics, associated information systems, business area development, skill development, and employee happiness.

Our take on happiness is a short quarterly survey, leading to close interactions with employees, installing a feel-good manager and allowing people to spend a certain budget at their own discretion on their own ideas (SMILE).

We are still improving every day and certainly didn't reach the end of what's possible, but we do indeed believe that this change in our focus is essential for our current and future success.

Changing Measurement Systems

So far, I mentioned information systems several times. The following chapters will dive a little bit deeper into numbers, focusing on success, happiness, and money. In phase one and two we used little to no data. Whatever was there existed in the form of spreadsheets, usually requiring a large amount of manual work. To still ensure the organization could operate, it was necessary to apply a huge amount of micromanagement on each and every employee. Due to the low focus of people filling management functions, most of this management was applied by a single high-level manager. This system clearly didn't scale. We realized this and starting with phase three, we installed better systems. Today we are still far from ideal, but at least we have some meaningful reports and one central information system providing data. It won't be long now before we reach a professional level there.

6.1 Measuring Success

In phase one and two, success was essentially measured in terms of money in the bank account. Only at the end of the year, when the financial statements were due, was additional information available. To manage day-to-day operations, the primary metric of days spent at the customer was used, measured in hours reported by the employee via a spreadsheet. Success was solely measured in monetary metrics—if at all. I was told the old CEO said that NovaTec wasn't around to earn money. No wonder success was an undefined term for us, if this quote is true!

Today, success consists of monetary goals, happiness goals, and strategic initiatives, both inside and outside competence areas, to develop new or existing business areas. Our competence area is a little bit ahead of the crowd in terms of quantified success criteria. While the overarching strategy is still in the works, let me show you what our CA strategy looks like.

Our competence area vision reads: "Together, discovering and creating a happier way of working." The motto associated with this vision is: "What if what you do matters?"

From this, we derived a strategy. It is valid for 1–5 years, depending on how quick we are in achieving it and how the market evolves. We defined four focus areas in our 2017 strategy: Happy customers, agile expertise at NovaTec, individual visibility, and competence area growth. Each of these areas has a defined goal, a target scenario description, and smaller sub-goals that can be reached within a shorter time span with a subset of the team.

The goal of "happy customers" is defined as: We want our customers to be happy with our work. Only then can we reach our vision and grow sustainably. Our good reputation defines us.

The target scenario is that all of our customers are very happy with our work (every NPS > 50%) and that we realize a contribution margin of 7–10% with our customers.

The sub-goals are:

- We have happy employees, because only these can create happy customers.
- We introduce account management to our competence area, but only for customers that are taken care of solely by us. This means that expectation management happens with every customer and customer surveys are conducted at least once per quarter via the consultant on site. If the results are below expectation (NPS < 50%), the competence area manager investigates.
- The projects of our customers are successful, whatever the customer defined as success criteria.
- The customer perceives our price-performance ratio as good. Therefore, we need to do market research about pricing and consulting categories (till March, then once per year) and define separate prices for different job categories. We establish the right price for the right job and person until the end of 2017, decrease our costs as far as possible (mindset), and make sure everybody is able to show at least one project from our strategic sectors in their project histories.
- We conduct more public Scrum Master trainings than last year.
- We focus on customers who are 1 h or less away (yellow zone) and are no more than 250 km away from where we live (red zone). We can serve these customers while sleeping in hotels less than five times per month (to be put in place by the end of 2018). These rules are not valid if there are no alternatives, strategic goals counter them, or we want the project for other reasons. The customer zones need to be visualized for the CA and sales, both for Stuttgart and relevant satellite sites.

The goal of "agile expertise" is defined as: We want our customers to perceive NovaTec as "agile." To achieve this, we need to live and demonstrate agile values and principles, both externally and internally.

The target scenario is that all employees at NovaTec are happy (average internal NPS > 50%) and describe their employer as being "agile" (>50% of employees asked).

The sub-goals are:

6.1 Measuring Success

- We try new approaches in our competence area that might benefit the company. We document our learnings and established a fuck-up-night at NovaTec [a term from the startup scene, meaning to make big failures transparent and learning from them]. New areas of agile business are continuously identified, evaluated, and developed, if relevant. To do this, we explicitly reserve time for this, established a bonkers day to get new ideas, teach our learnings regularly in a prioritized fashion, and check after every conference we visit if new topics could be relevant for us or are even "hot."
- We support leadership topics (career coaching and Management 3.0). Latest January 2019, career coaching must run self-sustained, without much support from our side. Until then, we focus on startup aid. This means we need to establish a standard career coaching training at NovaTec. Every leader was educated in Management 3.0 by the end of 2017 and exercises at least some of the practices in their specific areas of influence. To further push the topic, we need to establish a second Management 3.0 facilitator in 2018. Also, we are the contact for leaders within NovaTec for any questions regarding leadership.
- We support NovaTec with different agile topics. The primary focus are agile methods (Scrum, Kanban, etc.) and "New Work" topics, consisting primarily of "future workplace" and remote work. We advise as well as we can, but we do not accept accountability for other people's tasks. We continue to run our agile community of practice called "Agile Forum," as soon as at least five colleagues request it.
- We support customer projects in agile topics. This is primarily done by making sure every Scrum Master or Product Owner on a project meets our defined quality standards. In addition, we offer to support any NovaTec project with any customer with 5 days of coaching, if the costs are paid by the customer, directly or indirectly. The prerequisite for this is that our management board and our sales team know about this rule and put it into place.

The goal of "individual visibility" is defined as: We want every member of our team to be as visible in the market as they want to be, and as their salary level demands.

The target scenario is that our customers ask primarily for specific team members. The sub-goals are:

- We increase our external visibility, based on solid qualifications, in a way that makes the person more important than the position. Every individual achieves this by getting a baseline of 10–15 speaker engagements, adding at least two more per year. Everybody also authors a baseline of five professional articles and fifteen blog posts, adding two articles and four blog posts per year. On top of that, everybody needs public recommendations by customers, resulting in three or more appraisals and two or more case studies. These elements can be combined in different ways, while everybody needs to get at least 20 instances of visibility to attain a basic visibility in the market.

- We establish internal education by conducting bi-weekly learning sessions within the team. We also work together in every project. To achieve this, we find out when and how to pair, learn about the working models of our competitors, and do every second project as a full-time pair up to the end of 2017. These pairs are always paid for by the customer, except for new hires. To achieve this, we need to develop a line of argumentation, calculate our offers accordingly, and get customer feedback for reference. If we cannot be at the customers' sites together, we learn by collaborating on Fridays.

The goal of "competence area growth" is defined as: We want our sites in Frankfurt and Munich to act autonomously from our business unit's perspective. We also want to be able to serve all the customer requests we want to serve.

The target scenario is that in both sites we have at least five colleagues, the competence area is fully utilized with customer engagements and we can still serve 80% of incoming requests.

The sub-goals are:

- There are enough employees in all sites. We start with five team members both in Munich and Frankfurt, forming autonomous teams. To achieve this, we need to find out what growth rates are sustainable for us, especially in terms of contribution margins, seniority ratio, and special requirements of the sites.
- We put a recruiting strategy in place, for example covering the areas of conferences, customers, competition, and community.
- We know what we expect from new colleagues and documented this.
- We train at least one additional Scrum.org Professional Scrum Trainer.
- Our competence area functions as an interdisciplinary team. To achieve this, we create a matrix of required team competencies and make sure all identified aspects are covered by the team.

In creating this strategy, we tried to roughly follow the ideas of Tom Gilb (2005). The result is a quantification of all important goals, which is quite handy in determining what we achieved. We created this vision and strategy in a series of three half-day workshops, with a finishing touch by myself. We only managed to get there this quickly, because we share a high level of trust and a common purpose. In addition, we had failed at creating a strategy in the past. Our first attempt, back in phase one, was following a defined process for strategy creation, as defined in a book. We did not share the same purpose back then, resulting in 16 lengthy strategy workshops without any tangible result. At least we learned from this experience.

For our business unit, "success" is a defined concept with four different dimensions. Each dimension is measurable, so we know where we are at any time. NovaTec as such is still working on an overall strategy. However, we do have some goals today. These goals are focusing on financial returns and employee growth. The rest will follow soon. In my opinion, we are on the right track as a company and just need to continue the good work.

6.2 Measuring Happiness

As you could see in Sect. 5.3, happiness is immensely important for us. While this belief is as old as the competence area of agile methods, we only started measuring it across the company in phase three. We did some research and found many interesting models and surveys, all claiming to be a good indicator for employee satisfaction. Unfortunately, we were reluctant to ask a 100 questions or to focus on specific process areas some professor believed to be worth measuring. We believe focus will shift from one area of change to another, as people, market, and the enterprise develop. Therefore, we need a simple tool flexible enough to adapt continuously. We found it in the "Net Promoter Score" (NPS). It originally was intended to measure customer satisfaction and not employee happiness, but with servant leadership the employees are in some regards treated as the customers of your management. This was close enough for us, so we adopted the practice and experimented with the idea. We ask everybody each quarter: "How likely is it that you would recommend NovaTec to your friends?" The answer is given with a number on a 11-point scale. Below is another question, openly phrased: "Why did you choose this number?"

This open field gives us flexibility, because people will always enter what is bothering them most, no matter if we ask for it or not.

NPS functions in a very simple way. You count the total number of responses. The responses with nine and ten are called "promoters," the ones ranging from zero to six "detractors." People scoring in with seven or eight are considered neutral. You calculate the percentage of promoters and detract the percentage of detractors from it. The resulting net promoter score can vary between -100 and $+100$ (cf. Fig. 6.1).

Let's take a quick look at a simple example. Let's say 13 people answered the question. Four of them answered nine or ten, three of them between seven and eight, leaving six below seven. The NPS then is: $4/13 - 6/13 = -15.4\%$.

When we started measuring happiness, we did not know what to expect. The first data point, gathered from about a 100 respondents, produced a 15.2 result (cf. Fig. 6.2).

We were quite happy, started to act on the results and were startled when the second quarter we had dropped down to -5.5. The investigation showed that, on the one hand, people had not trusted the system to be anonymous and therefore chose higher numbers. On the other hand, the only reason people had actually realized that

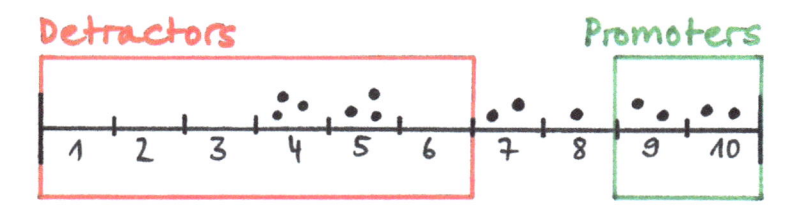

Fig. 6.1 Net promoter score distribution

Fig. 6.2 Net promoter score evolution at NovaTec

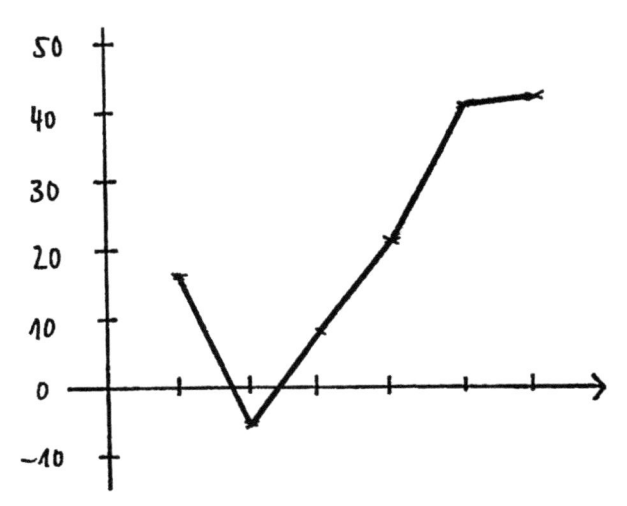

some things were going wrong was because we had done the survey. While in yearly questionnaires people forget what they answered from 1 year to the next, they tend to remember what they chose in a simple survey 3 months ago. Since no miracle had happened, solving all suggestions overnight, people had chosen lower scores. We took it as motivation and worked on the primary issues, resulting in improvements over time. After the fifth data point, we handed this survey over from our competence area to the HR department, because it was well-established and worked. The next two data points showed a near-stall in improvement rates and we are investigating what happened. It will be interesting to see if the next data point will remain stable, drop, or rise again. Whatever happens, it could either be coincidence or related to the shift in responsibility. We will observe and investigate.

If you are interested in a concrete example of how we analyzed the data, read on. If the following amount of numbers and tables inconveniences you, don't hesitate to jump to the next chapter.

To be able to analyze the data properly, we ask our respondents to fill in some additional fields. The first is if they are working as consultants or in one of the central departments. Secondly, we ask for the number of years they have been working with NovaTec. This is grouped (0–2 years, 3–5 years, 6–10 years, >10 years) so individuals can't be identified based on this selection. Lastly, we ask the respondents to tell us their career level (junior consultant to senior managing consultant or central departments). Together, this is interpreted. Take a look at the overall results from February 2017 (cf. Table 6.1):

About half of NovaTec's employees responded to the 1-week survey, which is a good response rate. Also, the overall number looks good with a happiness score of 41. Let's take a look if this is different for consultants and people working in central departments (cf. Table 6.2):

Interestingly, the happiness is almost the same for both domains. However, you can see that the central departments got there from zero happiness 3 months ago

6.2 Measuring Happiness

Table 6.1 Overall results

Total responses	105	100%
Promoters	54	51.4%
Detractors	11	10.5%
NPS		41%
Happiness index		41

Table 6.2 Results grouped by general domain

Area	Total	Promoters	Detractors	Happiness	Change since last survey
Consulting	97	50	10	41.2	+25.9
Central departments	8	4	1	37.5	+37.5

Table 6.3 Overall results grouped by tenure

Tenure	Total	Promoters	Detractors	Happiness	Change since last survey
0–2 years	40	26	3	57.5	+28.9
3–5 years	34	11	3	23.5	+20.7
6–10 years	18	10	3	38.9	+25.3
>10 years	13	7	2	38.5	+24.2

Table 6.4 Overall results grouped by career level

Career level	Total	Promoters	Detractors	Happiness	Change since last survey
Junior consultant	15	8	1	46.7	+4.6
Consultant	19	3	2	5.3	+31.2
Senior consultant	20	7	6	5.0	+5.0
Managing consultant	18	13	0	72.2	+42.2
Senior managing consultant	12	10	1	75.0	+15.0
Interns and students	13	9	0	69.2	+23.8
Central departments	8	4	1	37.5	+37.5

while the consultants already started from 15.3. Knowing the history, this was a huge jump in happiness for the central departments. Let's take a look if this is different based on how long people have been working with NovaTec (cf. Table 6.3):

Happiness rose almost the same through all groups. However, there are big differences. It looks like people having a history of 3–5 years with NovaTec are only about half as happy compared to people who just joined or stayed longer. If this is true, we should find a correlation with career levels, because people in that tenure group usually are "Consultant" or "Senior Consultant" (cf. Table 6.4).

Our theory seems to be valid. Consultants and Senior Consultants are least happy by far. Take a look at the Consultants: They rose to 5.3 from −26.9. Still, they are doing the worst in terms of happiness. Seeing these numbers, management knows on

Table 6.5 Criticism from the open text field

Career level	Number chosen	Criticism
Consultant	4	You can't question colleagues with higher seniority. If you want to deviate from their suggestions, you have to go through endless discussions or you just resign. Apart from this, the promotion policy is intransparent to me. I got the feeling that connections are more important than contributions.
Consultant	7	Work–life balance; salary could be higher
Consultant	7	The situation is good, but too vague when concerning the future.
Consultant	8	Not enough work–life balance if you don't work in one of the big projects.
Consultant	8	I don't want to do consulting work in the future, because I want to stop traveling.
Senior consultant	4	If you do consulting, you need to know what you get yourself into.
Senior consultant	4	The way employees on satellite sites were treated was off-limits. We were confronted with decisions already made without being able to contribute. I am not happy with my new manager. I am very sorry that my old manager will leave the company now.
Senior consultant	6	I am unsure about how much I should work.
Senior consultant	8	Exceptions from good rules, e.g. • Travel time from home to office is deducted from total travel time. • You only get bonus payments for days in the office, so you earn less when you are sick or taking leave. • Salary is below market average. • The brand definition has already taken more than a year. • Transparency is introduced too slowly.
Senior consultant	9	Small things don't match. For example, people not driving a company car get yearly increases in their car allowance while people driving a company car have to wait 3 years until they switch cars.

which people to focus. The open text comments can provide us with further insights. Let's take a look at the criticism of people being at the career level of "Consultant" or "Senior Consultant" right now and leave out all praise to not get ourselves into the feeling that we don't have to change anything (cf. Table 6.5).

To put these responses into perspective you should know that out of 105 respondents, 63 offered a comment. From the sample chosen above (Consultants and Senior Consultants), 21 out of 39 gave some textual feedback. Only 10 out of these 21 offered at least some criticism. These are what Table 6.5 shows.

As you can see, some people scoring high still have suggestions for improvements. The criticism can be clustered into five categories:

- Lack of leadership for the individual, leaving the person unsure about specific policies, unhappy in his project, or unclear about the "why" of decisions.
- People not being happy with the nature of consulting work.

- People unhappy with their salaries.
- People not being happy with specific company policies.
- People unhappy with the speed of change.

You probably already guessed that this survey was undertaken just after we changed the organizational structure, moving disciplinary leadership from department heads to competence area managers and totally failing at including the satellite sites. We tried to remedy this issue, but did not succeed everywhere.

Analyzing the other findings taught us some valuable insights. The first was that our leaders were not yet fully equipped to their (sometimes new) role. We needed to introduce some coaching for them and teach them how to coach their employees. Therefore, we introduced a coaching education program for them.

The second was that not everybody is happy with driving or flying around, doing consulting work. While this is a platitude, it was valuable for us to learn that the affected employees didn't know that they could switch projects to join one of the development activities that did not require them to travel. Again, a leadership issue, very similar to the third finding, which was the perceived unfairness of salaries.

We analyzed the market and individual salaries and found that in only very few cases did we have lower-than-average salaries. So, it was again a leadership issue, not putting the individual numbers into perspective for every employee.

The fourth finding was about the speed of change, which certainly could be far higher. For our management board, it was valuable to hear this criticism from the employee base and not only from their competence area managers. It gave them an additional boost.

The last finding was about specific company policies. These can be changed via SMILE (cf. Sect. 9.2), which means the unhappy colleagues were not aware of this system. Following this survey, we communicated the SMILE rules and contents several times to everybody through different channels to make sure everybody understood the system. Then, we waited to see if the same feedback popped up again.

6.3 Measuring Money

Money is certainly one criterion of success, equally important as employee happiness. Without happiness of employees, you won't earn money for long and without money, you won't have happy employees for long. One needs to find an equilibrium between these two criteria. Unfortunately, you can only manage things you measure, and in phase one there was no measurement of money in any way. This was inacceptable, so we started to measure some numbers within our business unit. We decided that two numbers were important, and two more needed to be present in order to calculate the first ones.

We defined the "contribution margin 1" (CM1) as the money left over after we deducted all direct variable costs from our revenue. These costs consist of project costs (train tickets, parking tickets, hotel fees, licensing fees, etc.), direct labor

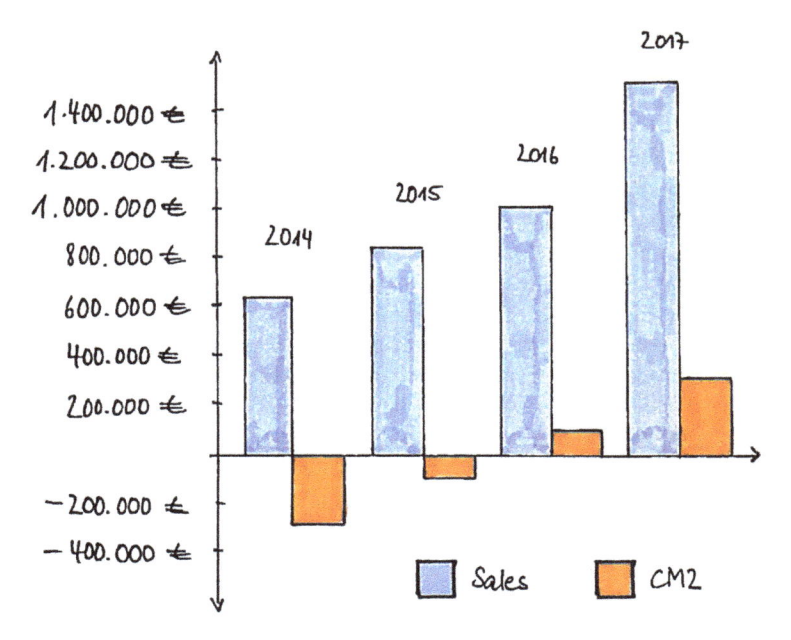

Fig. 6.3 Agile methods sales and earnings

expenses (salaries), and indirect labor expenses (taxes, fees, etc.). Basically, if an employee achieves a CM1 of zero, she earned her own salary.

We then continued to define the "contribution margin 2" (CM2) as the money left after the indirect costs are deducted from the CM1 as well. The indirect costs include office space, management salaries, central departments staff, etc. Basically, when somebody generates a CM2 above zero, she is earning money for the company.

In order to get to these CM1 and CM2 numbers, we needed to know our revenues and costs, the two supporting KPIs. This seems obvious today, but back in phase one the knowledge about sales and especially costs was a sacred cow. In our competence area, we quickly succeeded to understand our sales numbers, by simply just starting to write them down. During the first couple of months however, it was impossible to get figures for costs. The management board didn't want to disclose them. Only when we started to guess and then managed ourselves based on these guesses, did we receive some numbers in phase two. Today in phase three, every competence area manager receives automated reports for his business area and every single employee.

When you look at the numbers of our business area, you can see positive development of our results for the last couple of years. It is tempting to attribute these to the way we lead our employees. However, it is more likely that the general situation in the market combined with our focus on increasing the skills of our employees made all the difference. Whatever the true reason might be, it at least is obvious that we didn't harm our results by applying agile leadership. Figure 6.3 shows our numbers. 2014 is the first meaningful year for the purpose of this book,

6.3 Measuring Money

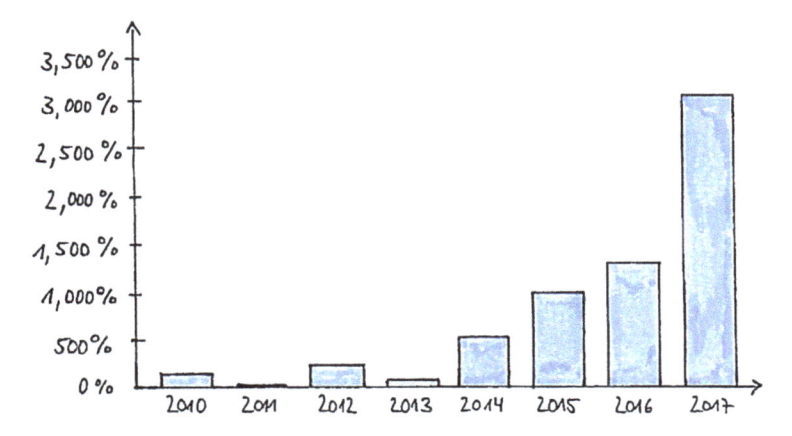

Fig. 6.4 Results per employee compared to 2010

because there are no numbers for the business area before that and we only started changing things at that time. My personal costs and returns are included, the numbers for 2017 are measured up to the end of the year. The numbers also include new employees, who usually learn for a couple of months before they start earning any money for the enterprise. If you want to take a look at detailed tables, please refer to the Appendix.

As you can see, we were coming from a startup situation, earning losses for the company, achieving break-even in year three and reaching a contribution margin of more than 22% in year four. These excellent numbers were possible because we focus uncompromisingly on skill growth of our team, leading to excellent agile coaches and trainers. However, this focus alone does not fully explain the numbers. The second reason which got us there is our public training portfolio combined with high market demand. Even though we don't accept more than 12–15 students in a single training, the contribution margin of these 2 days (which is the usual duration of our trainings) obviously increases with every additional paying customer.

It is worth taking a look at NovaTec's balance sheets of the last 7 years as well (cf. Fig. 6.4). Generalizing, phase two lasted from mid 2012 until May 2015, followed by phase three. I chose 2010 as a baseline (100%) because it is the year before I joined NovaTec. Showing percentages instead of absolute numbers eases interpretation.

Taking a look at phase one (2010–2012) and early phase two (2013), the volatility of results is apparent. A constant up and down, culminating in a struggle within the management board. During and after this struggle, results per employee started to increase steadily, going from 547% (2014) to 3111% (2017) of the 2010 numbers.

During the same period, we succeeded in reducing the number of days employees were engaged in customer work (cf. Fig. 6.5), which allows us to educate them better and enable them to do a better job for our customers.

Spending more time with NovaTec colleagues at the office is also a major contributor to employee happiness. Happiness, on the other hand, reduces employee

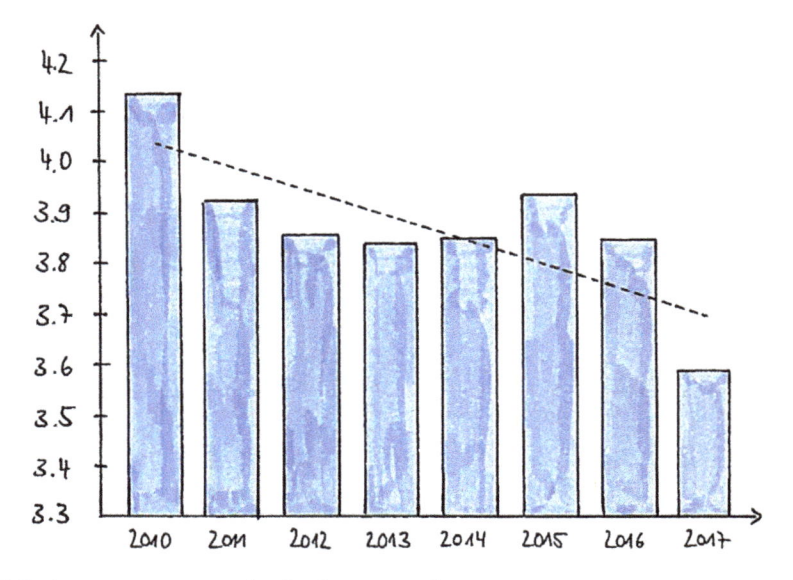

Fig. 6.5 Average customer productive days per week

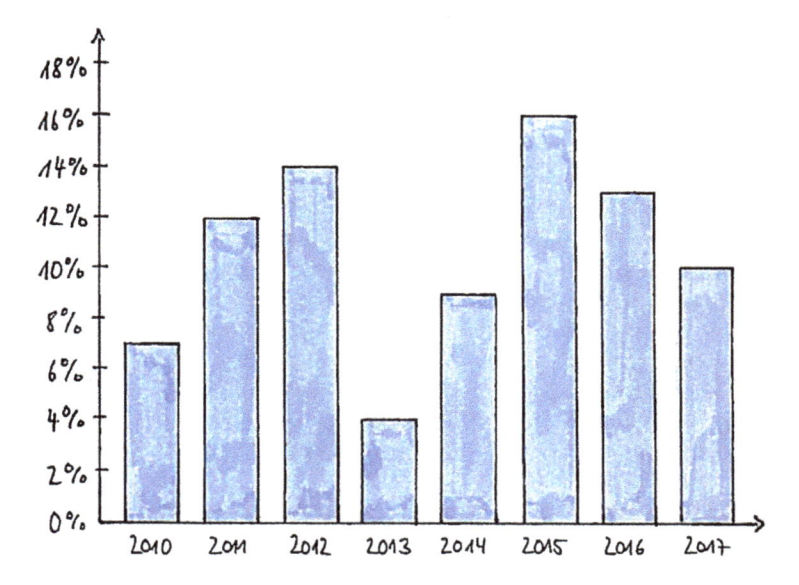

Fig. 6.6 Employee turnover (percentage of staff)

turnover, which is also evident at NovaTec since we changed our focus early in phase three. Of course, you also see the huge impact of our phase two struggles (cf. Fig. 6.6).

Reducing the average number of days an employee earns money by working with customers from 4.14 (2010) to 3.59 (2017) means we are earning more money with less hours spent in projects. Imagine: 31 times the result of 2010! This all depends on the absolute numbers in 2010 of course, and these were fairly low. It is also meaningful to take a look at the year on year financial growth rate. Again, there was a huge volatility before phase three. Today, there is steady growth of 72% (2015), 71% (2016), and 93% (2017), year on year. We are now reaching a natural cap with our numbers because our business model depends on the hours and days a person works, and this number is limited. We expect the growth rate to drop down to a number linearly correlated to our employee growth. Also, the 2017 result was only achieved by an extraordinary effort made by all employees in the fourth quarter. We were at risk of missing the 2016 result in 2017, because we changed a policy and initially didn't keep up with our leadership efforts.

Up until 2016 we didn't pay out overtime and we only allowed people to reduce a small amount of overtime by taking days off. Based on employee feedback, we changed this policy in 2017, essentially telling our competence area managers that they could decide on overtime leave themselves, as long as their financials supported this. This policy change contributed to a steep increase in employee happiness. Unfortunately, we didn't provide our managers with the numbers to manage the situation soon enough. The policy changed in January, but they only received numbers in July. In addition, the skill to interpret these numbers needed some honing, which takes time. During that time, most leave requests from employees were just granted without a second thought. To make matters worse, we had not agreed on target results for all business units in relation to each other, leading to a misleading local focus from everybody involved. When we realized things were moving into the wrong direction (meaning people didn't work enough on customer projects but instead on internal activities), we asked all employees to make an extra effort for the last months of the year. They did, and we not only achieved our goal, we even exceeded it.

The good thing about this mistake is the tremendous amount of learning we achieved. People today better understand the impact of their behavior on their numbers. While in January the term "C-Prod" (average customer days per week) was unknown to almost everybody, today everyone knows what the impact of changing even a small fraction of this number means for them and the company. Also, people largely behave responsibly when it comes to taking leave. For example, some managers feared employees might do a lot of overtime during the year and then collectively stay home for several weeks during Christmas, stripping our customers bare of support and reducing our profit margins. This didn't happen. Only very few individuals took an imbalanced approach between their individual needs and NovaTec.

What we will change next is to define interrelated goals, and to break down individual targets based on these goals. We will also continue to experiment with the optimal value for "C-Prod." We want to achieve both good financial results and enough time for employees to work on developing their skills to keep up with the needs of our customers.

6.4 Learnings

We defined and quantified common goals and learned to focus on information systems to measure monetary success. This included getting away from spreadsheets and toward an ERP system with automated reports. This approach scales unlike manually digging up individual numbers from outdated spreadsheets. We are still improving this system every day and while we are still far from the end we will soon have reached a competitive level.

The basis for measuring company-wide success today are monetary goals, employee happiness goals, and strategic initiatives, both inside and outside competence areas, to develop new business areas. Our competence area of agile methods is a little bit ahead of the crowd in terms of quantified success criteria, and we broke down the more general overarching goals into more specific ones for ourselves.

Measuring employee happiness across the organization became one of the primary metrics for us. Instead of lengthy yearly questionnaires, we chose to work with simple quarterly check-ups. In our case, a net promoter score augmented by an open text field does the job. When we started the measurements, there was an initial drop in happiness. The reason was that while in yearly questionnaires people forget what they answered from one occurrence to the next, they tend to remember what they chose in some simple survey 3 months ago and therefore notice if their improvement request was acted upon or not.

Without happiness of employees, you won't earn money for long and without money, you won't have happy employees for long. This is the reason why contribution margins are our primary financial metric at the moment, and equally important to us as employee happiness. Providing automated reports with monetary information is our standard today, but we had to butcher the sacred cow of "information monopolies" to get there. Our numbers show that we didn't harm our results by applying agile leadership, even though it is not easy to draw a linear conclusion from our actions to success. There are many market variables we cannot control which are also very relevant. However, our phase three results are excellent. We take this as evidence that our approach is working and will continue to refine it.

Changing Reward Systems

When we started changing our processes and shifted the focus toward our employees, we also realized that we had to change our reward systems. Before we start thinking about who rewards whom, we have to answer the fundamental question: What are rewards?

7.1 What Are Rewards?

Most people believe that rewards are money and promotions. However, this is not the complete story. While money is important for everybody, promotions are not. Recognition however is very relevant for almost everyone (see Kudo Cards, Sect. 2.4). As you could see earlier (cf. Sect. 2.2), Moving Motivators is a great Management 3.0 technique to find out what really motivates an individual. Because of these individual needs, rewards need to come in many facets. For some people, trying new projects or roles is more important than earning an additional sum of money. For others, being publicly lauded does the trick. Some crave for new titles (maybe even invented by themselves), others want to be requested by a certain team or want to be given the freedom to make certain decisions alone. Some people even consider being left alone as being rewarded.

Don't get me wrong: Money is and stays important. People need to consider their salary as being "fair." But once this level is reached, it depends very much on the person as to which reward is the most effective and appreciated, while the motivating effects of pay rises wear off quickly. To accommodate this, we started to add Moving Motivators to our library of management tools and use it every now and then to get to know our employees better. In our business area, we did it collectively once and now use it in development dialogues whenever it feels appropriate. For me, the rule of thumb is: If I can't tell you what kind of recognition an employee would appreciate most, I will suggest trying Moving Motivators during one of our next one-on-one sessions.

7.2 Who Gets Rewarded How by Whom

At NovaTec, we institutionalized a multitude of rewards. In many cases, we didn't even recognize them as rewards before we started looking more closely at the topic. On the peer level, we use Kudo Cards, Bonusly, personal praise, individual tokens of appreciation (e.g., cookies), chief fun officer, pair working, and SMILE.

We already discussed Kudo Cards and Bonusly in Sect. 2.4. Together with direct praise offered through personal means like a chat message or cookies for somebody, they are the foundation of peer-level rewards. All of them are unidirectional, so each person can decide to give a reward without the receivers being required to do anything on their own. The other rewards work in both directions, meaning some sort of consensus or action is required by both sender and receiver. For example, our "chief fun officer" is institutionalized only within our business unit and rotates through the team (cf. Sect. 2.1). If she wants to organize a team event, which is often (at least partly) paid for by the participants themselves and takes place in peoples' spare time, she will need the consensus of everyone in the team. Even when the company pays for the event, it is a sign of appreciation when everybody invests time with their colleagues. Another reward, at least for some people, is the ability to co-work with other people at the customer. Usually, the customer only pays for one consultant on-site, or we use one trainer to deliver a training. If a team member decides to pair, this effectively means that his contribution margin will be lower than possible for this engagement, which can mean that he will have to work longer hours on other engagements to make up for the difference. The same effect is true for both people pairing. When they decide to do this, it is a reward for both by both. It also is a commitment to learning and improving. Last but not least, as you already know we have a system called "SMILE" in place. It is a system for employees to suggest improvements, to jointly decide about these improvements, and to implement them. You can read more about the details about it in Sect. 9.2. If the suggestion of a specific employee or group is put into practice, this very often is perceived as a reward by the one suggesting the change. In every case, it is a cross-department form of appreciation to even discuss ideas, all the more allowing them to come to life.

On the boss-worker level, we use praise, pay rises, bonus payments, promotions, titles, off-the-job training, engaging renowned experts for in-house trainings, professional offsite events, career coaching, parties, delegation of power, stable teams and letting employees choose their own projects.

Praise can come in many forms. In my case, most of it comes in transparent ways openly in front of the team, sent via email to the team, or written into the team chat. On some occasions, especially if the incident is especially noteworthy, I choose a more private setting and explain the reason for my praise in detail. From my personal point of view, this shows appreciation, because time is the most valuable resource I am able to spend. Most of my team mates share this view.

Pay rises, bonuses, promotions, and granting titles that go along with career paths is the traditional way I can use to reward employees. We try not to overemphasize these options and only do them once a year. It is noteworthy that with my team they don't work very well either. Yes, some of them love titles and everybody likes to receive a higher pay, but these are not preferred options. For example, I awarded two people a special bonus this year. One of them said "thank you" (and that was it) and the other one didn't even notice the additional four-digit-number and instead dove deep into some detail of his salary calculation that could (but most likely won't) make a difference of about €200 next year. In another case, I provided an employee with an expensive bottle of wine. This person likes wine and was very happy to receive this special bottle. There was real joy in his face and I got the feeling that he appreciated the gesture. This taught me a valuable lesson: I will never again award monetary bonuses in an impersonal way. Instead, I will try to show my appreciation through other means, depending on the hobbies and tastes of my employees, or bring cash to the meeting (which might prove difficult in terms of compliance—I haven't tried that one yet). Both of us will benefit from this more personal approach.

Something that is better received by our team is honing skills through off-the-job training, doing certain workshops offsite instead of in our own meeting rooms, or renting renowned experts for in-house trainings. All these options show our employees that we appreciate their skills and are willing to invest even more time and money into them. Being consultants, this is also highly relevant for what we do. In addition, flying in top-tier experts from all over the world allows us to let special customers join the experience. All sorts of educational events are in high demand, leading me to often overspending our educational budget. I am very glad that we don't take budgets as carved in stone but rather as a guideline we should only step across with good reason.

As a consequence, it is normal for some of our employees to participate in two to four trainings each year or fly across the world to attend special conferences. The drawback of this practice is that some people, who have never worked with another employer, take this for granted and don't appreciate it as a reward system. They rather believe to have a right to demand even more. I didn't find an easy way out of this trap yet. These people probably need to test other waters first before they start to value corporate educational support.

A very special element of our reward system can be argued about. Career coaching, that is providing internal professional coaches to support our employees with their career development through coaching and mentoring, is an extension of traditional development dialogues. While every employee should have such dialogues regularly and often, most companies I know only do them once a year. In addition, they usually don't provide any coaching techniques that actually help the coachee to develop herself during the session and beyond. It is a huge difference if you collect wishes from your employees, grant a training, and are done for the year, or if you help your employee to reach a new level of self-awareness that leads her to uncover previously unknown potential. Therefore, career coaching is part of our reward system from my point of view. It very often is delivered by peers of the coachees, but it is a service offered by the manager.

Something you probably have experienced many times yourself are parties. They are relatively easy to implement (grant money, usually there is somebody who wants to organize the event) and can show appreciation on project, business unit, or company level. We institutionalized a certain budget for this type of reward and called it "pizza money." Whenever a manager wants to thank his team with a party, free food, or similar, we just do it. There is no need for lengthy approval processes. We also conduct additional parties on a larger scale, but more of that later.

The last elements of boss-to-worker rewards I want to highlight are delegation of power and stable teams. You can read more about delegation in Sect. 9.1. For now, it suffices to say that we think very carefully about which power to delegate to whom and we try to push decisions down the lines to the people who are most affected by them. For example, hiring new people into our team needs a consensus between our team and myself. I cannot hire without the team's consent. This also affects daily work, for example by allowing people to choose their own projects (cf. Sect. 9.3) instead of imposing this from the top. "Stable teams" is a very specific aspect of power. In some companies, people are viewed as "resources" that can be switched, changed, and mixed easily. This doesn't show respect or appreciation and is certainly not a reward. "Thank you for your good work, let me change your social working environment again for you to see if you can still succeed this time" is no message we want to send. Therefore, we try to keep teams stable for as long as possible. In our competence areas that works like a charm. People appreciate having a "home" and knowing where they belong. They also appreciate that it is their choice if they want to stay in this team or leave it.

Let's take a look at the real "top-down" rewards. These are the ones issued to the employees by our management board. On this level, we use company-wide training programs, long-term educational programs, contract adjustments, creation of new satellite sites, new roles and titles, corporate cars, company-wide bonuses, company-wide parties, recognition at certain events, budgets for new ideas, and state-of-the-art working equipment.

Since education is a vital part of our business and professional growth, we value it everywhere, including board level. Here we provide essentially two facets of education: a company-wide training program and special grants for long-term educational programs. The training program as such is focused on the skills we need as consultants, mainly covering soft and language skills since hard skill needs vary widely and are delivered by the competence areas. Every employee can take part in these classes, ranging from business etiquette through presentation and rhetorical skills, to business English and labor law. Every employee can participate and while the competence area managers officially have the right to veto individual participation, I do not know of a single case where that happened, unless the employee already had handed in his resignation.

The special grants for long-term educational programs are not so easy to get. For exceptional employees who express interest in further education such as a master's degree program, a 2-year coaching program or writing a doctoral thesis, the board supports them with time, money, or both. Study fees can be substantial and in these cases are covered in full by the enterprise. In some cases, working hours can be used to study. Even though this is usually only a fraction of the total time required, it comes in quite handy to leave the office early on Fridays to get to university in time—and still be paid for it. Personally, I received a monetary grant to do my MBA. The costs were almost fully covered, but I didn't ask for time, so I studied on weekends and evenings. When somebody gets such a grant, they are usually asked to commit themselves to stay in the company for at least a couple of more years so they can put their newly learned skills to good use for our customers, although with this group of employees such measures are actually not necessary. They would do this anyway.

When personal circumstances change, your job expectations might change as well. Valued employees (which is almost everybody at NovaTec) can then ask for contract adjustments. This includes moving to a different office in another town or adjusting the required number of working hours per week. Both options are handled without bureaucracy. It only gets difficult if the town you want to move to doesn't have a branch office yet. However, if you are a top-tier employee and the board trusts you in building up and running a satellite site yourself, you can just open up a new one—with the full support of the board, of course. You would then also be awarded the new title of "branch office manager." This title, as well as the title of "competence area manager" is only assigned by the board, which makes sense since these are strategically relevant positions for NovaTec. In addition to these, from time to time the board allows employees to choose new titles for themselves. For example, one seasoned consultant dug deep into the topic of employee happiness and subsequently suggested to be awarded the title of "feel-good manager." His request was granted, alongside with a portion of time (2–3 days per week) that he can now use to push the topic forward within the company. While such new roles are invented rarely, they do have a significant impact on the people affected and are definitely perceived as a reward.

Something that is more common is our corporate car policy. Every consultant has a certain budget, depending on her career level, which she can use every 3 years to order a new car. There are some rules that must be followed, governing aspects like engine horse power, model type, or color. As long as people stay within this policy, they are free to choose whatever they like. Deviations from these rules are possible as well. Depending on your tenure with the company, even big exceptions can be made. Of course, employees have to cover the additional expenses by themselves, but for some of them driving a bigger car is worth the additional cost. For others, big cars are actually a drawback. At the moment, the board is working on a rule that incentivizes leasing smaller cars by paying out the difference to their allowance to the employees (this was a SMILE idea by the way). We hope to make a contribution to our environment and satisfy all needs this way.

If people don't choose a car, they get more money each month that covers their additional expenses to use their own cars to get to our customers. This means that almost everybody in the company has access to this reward in one way or another.

Accessibility is also true for the following rewards: bonuses, parties, public recognition, and budgets for new ideas. If NovaTec performs well during a year, very often a larger fraction of the profit is paid back to the employees. There are only very few occasions where individual bonuses are paid out by the board. Usually, the decision about bonus payments lies with the competence area managers. This strengthens the collective spirit of everybody with leadership responsibility. If the company thrives, employees thrive as well.

The collective spirit is also fostered through parties. There are at least two of them each year: A summer party for employees and their families, and a Christmas party just for the employees. The company invests heavily in them and even pays for accommodation if you need it. Work hard, play hard. At these (and other) events, some employees are publicly lauded if they achieved something extraordinary that year. Always with a personal touch and often with a joking twist to it. For example, at one Christmas party I was praised for the work I had done that year in the agile domain. While being lauded, a picture of me, merged with one of Master Yoda, was shown, causing a good laugh in the audience. I still remember that situation with a smile, so do many of my colleagues, to the extent that it is still used often today.

The most powerful reward (at least from my perspective) the board has at their disposal is the distribution of additional budget for new ideas. If somebody has a great idea and the board believes this employee can bring it to life, there is a flexible amount of money available for it. For example, our employee suggestion and improvement system SMILE (cf. Sect. 9.2) was created in this way, supplied with a yearly budget of 50.000€ in 2017 (this should rise with increases in employee numbers). Other ideas received less or no money but are nevertheless supported with time, organization, equipment, food, or similar things: Founding a local Toastmasters group, conducting sessions on mindfulness, playing games all night several times a year and going skiing or hiking with everybody who likes to participate are just some examples of what we brought to life. While not everybody makes use of these rewards, they are well-known and highly valued throughout the company.

The last reward I want to mention here is state-of-the-art working equipment. For technology-savvy people like us, this is important. We can choose between different brands of smartphones and laptops in excellent configurations. In addition to business use, we can also use them for private needs. After some years (two for phones, three for laptops) we get new equipment and can buy the old equipment for a reduced price.

As you can see, we offer a wide range of rewards. Depending on each individual person, some resonate more than others. One explanation is that everybody has different priorities in their intrinsic motivators. Table 7.1 provides you with an overview of the rewards mentioned above, clustered by hierarchy level and mapped to the ten intrinsic motivators of Management 3.0 (refer to Sect. 2.2 for details) influenced by them. Of course, this is just my perception, your individual mapping might be different.

As you can see, all ten intrinsic motivators described in Management 3.0 are covered by some sort of reward, with some being covered more extensively than others. There are two major things I learned from analyzing our reward system: Firstly, little rewards coming from the heart beat big rewards that are institutionalized. Secondly, rewards wrapped into gamification have a more lasting effect than the ones without gamification elements. At NovaTec, we definitely need more gamification. This is what we will work on next in this domain.

7.2 Who Gets Rewarded How by Whom

Table 7.1 Rewards mapped to intrinsic Management 3.0 motivators

Reward	Hierarchy level	Management 3.0 motivators influenced
Kudo Cards	Peers	Acceptance, honor, relatedness
Bonusly	Peers	Acceptance, honor, relatedness
Personal praise	Peers	Acceptance, relatedness
Individual tokens of appreciation	Peers	Acceptance, relatedness
Chief fun officer	Peers	Relatedness
Pair working	Peers	Acceptance, curiosity, mastery, relatedness
SMILE	Peers	Freedom, goal, power, status
Praise	Boss-worker	Acceptance, relatedness
Pay rises	Boss-worker	Status
Bonus payments	Boss-worker	Status
Promotions	Boss-worker	Status
Titles	Boss-worker	Status
Off-the-job training and conference visits	Boss-worker	Freedom, goal, mastery, status
Renting renown experts for in-house trainings	Boss-worker	Goal, mastery, status
Professional offsite events	Boss-worker	Mastery, relatedness, status
Career coaching	Boss-worker	Acceptance, curiosity, freedom, goal, honor, mastery, relatedness
Parties	Boss-worker	Relatedness
Delegation of power	Boss-worker	Freedom, order, power, status
Stable teams	Boss-worker	Acceptance, order, power, relatedness
Letting employees choose their own projects	Boss-worker	Curiosity, freedom, order, power, status
Company-wide training programs	Management board-worker	Goal, mastery, order
Long-term educational programs	Management board-worker	Freedom, goal, mastery, status
Contract adjustments	Management board-worker	Freedom, goal
Creation of new satellite sites	Management board-worker	Freedom, goal, status
New roles and titles	Management board-worker	Acceptance, curiosity, freedom, goal, honor, power, status
Corporate cars and exceptions	Management board-worker	Status
Company-wide bonuses	Management board-worker	Order, relatedness
Company-wide parties	Management board-worker	Acceptance, relatedness
Recognition at certain events	Management board-worker	Acceptance, status

(continued)

Table 7.1 (continued)

Reward	Hierarchy level	Management 3.0 motivators influenced
Budgets for new ideas	Management board-worker	Acceptance, curiosity, goal, honor, power, status
State-of-the-art equipment	Management board-worker	Status

7.3 Salary Systems

Salaries are governed by a standardized compensation plan at NovaTec. The basic structure is a fixed amount of money, a variable portion granted for "productive work," plus your car or the respective amount paid out as "car allowance." Everybody has more or less the same compensation plan, the only things that vary are the numbers and the distribution between fixed and variable pay. It is also interesting to take a closer look at what is defined as "productive work." In phase one, this was the billable time spent working for customers. This meant for every hour at a customer project, the employee would receive additional money, while helping to improve NovaTec, creating new products or improving one's own skills were not gratified. The message was clear: All employees were valued less for sharpening the axe than for cutting down trees. This led to some colleagues effectively stopping every type of work that was not customer billable. In phase two, we changed this, allowing competence area managers to define other work as "productive" as well. Officially, this meant every task each employee did had to be evaluated by the accountable competence area manager, followed by a formal classification of the work. In practice, the managers didn't have the time to do this, so they switched the mode to automatically granting every hour worked for competence area topics as being "productive." Only when exceptions occurred, we deviated from this practice. For example, individuals who did not produce any results and were not working for customers were exempt from this rule. In one case, my team collectively decided to opt out from paying out competence area bonus money, because our numbers were not good enough and we believed it not to be fair if we asked for even more money. A nice side effect of having transparent numbers. In phase three, we switched the mode company-wide to declare every hour, no matter what was done, to automatically be productive. There are only three exceptions from this rule today: If a competence area manager decides to make an exception, travel time and time not working (holidays, sickness, etc.). The message this sends is: "We value your work, no matter what you do." This comes very close to fixed-pay contracts. What is still keeping the board from removing the variable portion in the paperwork is the fear that people could stop doing overtime if they no longer receive their productivity bonus, or people might feel treated unfairly if they do overtime and didn't get additional money for it.

The amount of money somebody receives is closely aligned with people's career levels. While officially no correlation exists, it is quite obvious. Also, whenever a specific salary is decided on, it is compared to people on the same career level with similar experience. The result is a set of salary bandwidths aligned with career levels, exposing blurred edges. A career level—let's say becoming a "Senior Consultant"—depends on the candidate's expertise and experience. In my opinion, this set of dependencies would allow us to create some sort of transparent salary formula to stop the yearly fuss about pay rises, but this is still the minority opinion in the company. There is also a huge unresolved conflict in the enterprise: What is fairness? Some people believe it is fair to pay the same amount of money if people have the same amount of experience and are at the same career level. Others believe the value produced for the company should play a dominant role in determining salaries, leading to experience and career level taking a back seat. Keeping salaries hidden means that this conflict continues to exist. It also removes the necessity to solve it. Solving it would mean taking a clear stance as a company, probably leading to many people leaving the enterprise. It also would make legacy imbalances obvious. In Germany, it is almost impossible to cut somebody's salary, even for poor performance. Once you paid a certain amount, you have to stick with it forever. While transparent salaries would remove the risk of wrong decisions in the future, past mistakes would be painfully visible. We already started to address this issue, but this takes time and in some cases is impossible to solve without firing the person, which is also difficult in Germany.

From my point of view, correcting our legacy salary system and deciding on a clear path for the future is one of our main challenges for the upcoming years. My dream is a transparent salary formula that accounts for performance. For me, this is the fairest option, at the same time minimizing the need for actively managing individual salaries. Let's see if it will stay a dream.

7.4 Learnings

Rewards come in many forms and are perceived very differently depending on the person receiving it. While in earlier days the primary rewards consisted of promotions and money, today individual needs require individualized rewards. Money remains important of course, but only to a certain degree. A good way to figure out the preferences of your employees is the Management 3.0 practice of Moving Motivators.

We installed a variety of rewards. Some of them can be dispensed by peers, some of them by the disciplinary manager, and some of them can only be distributed by the management board. Some of them work across department boundaries, some of them don't. For me, time spent is the most valuable form of appreciation since time is the most valuable resource I possess. This also means that rewards associated with money are usually less effective than the ones that take a personal effort to create. Basically, little rewards coming from the heart beat big rewards that are institutionalized. Also, gamification has a positive impact on the effectiveness of rewards.

Our salary system is evolving slowly and consists of a fixed portion, variable pay for "productive work," and a company car. People's pay depends on their career level, which depends on their expertise and experience. Our system is working well, but causes a lot of management effort each year. We do not have a transparent salary formula yet, because we still have the legacy of past wrong decisions. There is also an unresolved conflict about whether it is fair to include value produced into the decision process, or if the same amount of experience and career level should be enough. Therefore, our salaries are not yet transparent. Resolving this is one of our biggest challenges for the upcoming years.

Changing Career Paths

Career paths are important enough to dedicate a major chapter to them. On the one hand, our employees expressed the need for a more nuanced career model, which I will outline to you. On the other hand, the meaning of "career" is changing fundamentally (cf. Fig. 8.1). In earlier days, it was quite clear that "career" meant rising up through the ranks, step by step, up the pyramid. Today, people might as well want to grow horizontally, depending on their individual needs, or skip a step. For example, I offered two of my team mates to try the role of "competence area manager," or at least aim for it in the long run. They refused, emphasizing that their preference for a coaching leadership stance would not be possible when considering the disciplinary parts of the role, such as deciding on salaries, handling escalations, or monitoring business results.

In the past, we only had one career path. We didn't think about it much, it was just there. Only when we installed an additional career path last year, did we name this traditional path "consulting career." The new path is a "specialist career," which will be outlined in the next chapters. Of course, we handle these two flexibly, using our common sense. You will also find a chapter called "Management Career," which is basically a special manifestation of the specialist career.

8.1 Consulting Career

A consultant helps customers with knowledge and skills not available at the customer themselves. This can take on many forms, but usually it is a mixture of teaching, providing advice, and doing the job yourself. This includes highlighting areas to the customer where more consulting could be helpful, which is a form of selling. The more experienced a consultant is, the better she is able to spot gaps in the organization of her customers, and to fill more of these herself. For us, this resulted in the career levels as described in Table 8.1.

To advance through these levels was a very rigid and nevertheless unpredictable process in phase one. Back then, a multitude of assessment criteria in lengthy

Fig. 8.1 Career models are changing

Table 8.1 NovaTec career levels

Career level	Junior consultant	Consultant	Senior consultant	Managing consultant	Senior managing consultant
Abbreviation	JC	C	SC	MC	SMC

spreadsheets had to be filled in. Then, the employee's disciplinary manager had to issue a recommendation for promotion, which was sent to the management board. The management board then decided whether to promote the employee—or not. The feedback was provided back to the disciplinary manager, who then had to share the result with the employee. While this was easy for the levels up to Senior Consultant, it became quite difficult the further up the career ladder you went. Basically, if you didn't succeed in creating a positive image of yourself at board level, you had no chance of being promoted.

Today, we have a shortened list of criteria (cf. Table 8.2) that is far more relevant than our spreadsheet-frenzy back in phase one. Still, favoritism plays a role, but at least now the criteria for it are transparent. The following table shows which criteria are relevant and to which extent in order to be promoted to the corresponding level. The criteria are additive, so a Senior Managing Consultant will need to exhibit all the skills Junior Consultants to Managing Consultants need, plus whatever is special for the SMC level.

Even though this is hard to believe, the criteria above are a shortened and more transparent list compared to what we had in phases one and two. Some criteria can still be interpreted in different ways, but most of them are well defined in our internal wiki system. The most interesting aspect can be found in the first line. It's the connection of career and competency level.

8.2 Specialist Career

Many people at NovaTec did not accept the model above when we made it transparent. Even though all relevant criteria were now clear, some people didn't want to fulfill them. This was especially true for the sales aspects of the job. We also realized that we have a couple of employees who are happiest if they never meet a

8.2 Specialist Career

Table 8.2 Promotion criteria at NovaTec (consulting career)

Competency level	JC	C Adept	SC Practitioner	MC Expert	MC	SMC Lead
Business development & project sales	–	Rarely helps out	Occasionally supports sales tasks	Distinct: uncovers new opportunities and highlights them to the sales team, supports acquisition tasks actively from a business perspective		Particularly strong: is responsible for sales at the front line, negotiates with customers, pushes acquisitions forward
Economic complexities	–	Basic understanding	Deep understanding on project level	Deep understanding on business unit level		Deep understanding on corporate level
Self-reliance	Is always being managed	Is largely being managed	Is working self-managed, alone or in the team	Is working self-managed, alone or in the team		Is working self-managed, alone or in the team
Responsibility	Own work	Own work	Manages a team or subproject	Manages a project		Manages customers on program level
Coaching of colleagues on the job	No	Rarely	Yes	Yes		Yes
Mentoring of colleagues on the job	No	Rarely	Yes	Yes		Yes
In customer contexts talks to	Experts	Experts	Lower level managers	Lower level managers		Higher level managers
Customer visibility	Low, hardly ever personally visible	Low, hardly ever personally visible	High, is being perceived as "Senior Consultant"	Very high, is being perceived as "Managing Consultant"		Extremely high, is being perceived as "Senior Managing Consultant"
Understanding, collecting, and pushing customer needs	Operative	Operative	Operative & strategically	Strategically & operative		Strategically
	Small	Small to medium	Medium	High		Very high

(continued)

Table 8.2 (continued)

	JC	C	SC	MC	SMC
Contribution to competence area development					
Trainings	Contributes to training program development	Contributes to training program development and conducts training	Contributes to training program development and conducts training	Contributes to training program development and conducts training	Contributes to training program development and conducts training
Publications	–	Writes blog posts	Writes blog posts	Writes blog posts	Writes blog posts
Conferences	–	Visits conferences	Visits conferences	Visits conferences	Visits conferences
Assets and frameworks	–	Contributes to asset development	Provides input for asset development from a business perspective	Provides input for asset development from a business perspective	Provides input for asset development from a business perspective
Community activity and public events	–	–	Co-shape events	Planning and conducting events	Planning and conducting events
Communication skills (facilitation, rhetoric, presentation, negotiation)	–	Facilitation and presentation	Facilitation and presentation	Rhetoric and negotiation skills	Excellent negotiation skills
Servant leadership	–	Know what it is	Know what it is	Live it in your management role	Exhibit it in everything you do
Personal traits (empathy, reliability, flexibility, readiness to help others, enthusiasm, working out ones conflicts)	Present	Present	Visible	Role model	Role model
Personal skills (working with others, communication, giving and receiving criticism, managing conflict	Present	Present	Visible	Role model	Role model

8.2 Specialist Career

situations, honesty, assertiveness, persuasiveness, customer focus, self-organization, self-confidence, integrity, structured thinking)	Present	Present	Visible	Role model
Personal attitude (punctuality, engagement, team focus, solution-orientation)	Know some of these	Know some of these	Know some of these	Role model
Process and tool know-how (requirements engineering, software development tools, project management, software architecture, product testing, quality management, engineering practices)		Know some of these	Know many of these	Know many of these

customer in a selling context. They don't want to do the traditional "consulting pitch," they want to rely on their own proven abilities and track results as their personal sales pitch. Therefore, we introduced a specialist career in phase three. Most aspects of our consulting career remain unchanged, but some elements changed considerably. Table 8.3 shows the deviations of this career path compared to Table 8.2.

Simplifying it, the difference is that we expect people in the specialist career path to be the extraordinarily competent face of NovaTec to the outside world while people in the consulting career path have to do an extraordinary sales job. Both paths are tied to technical competency, the difference is how much of it must be shown on stage and in articles. The competency levels mentioned in Table 8.2 are defined within the competence areas and are very specific to the area of expertise the employees are working in.

In our competence area of agile methods, we decided to create a skill definition earlier. Our purpose was to provide a learning path to all employees who wanted to gain expertise in our domain. Therefore, we defined skill levels back in phase one, continually refined it, and still use them. It is very handy to use this as a rough framework in our development dialogues, or when an employee is thinking about what step to take next.

We created a framework (which is basically a competency matrix, cf. Management3.0h) with the following areas: Agile Organizational Development, Kanban, Scrum Product Owner, Scrum Master and Trainer. Table 8.4 shows the current state of our competence definition for Scrum Masters within this framework.

You can see that there are some cross-references to other competency definitions, especially "Agile Organizational Development." This means somebody wanting to reach the next level as a Scrum Master will need to deep dive into organizational development as well. Also, some aspects (such as Scrum experience) seem to be low bars. In practice, this doesn't play a big role, because other aspects are more important. We don't want to punish somebody who puts a lot of effort into it while at the same time we don't want to favor somebody who just does his time. If you excel, you will deliver more value sooner and rise through this model quickly.

The next refinement for this framework is overdue, but it is still a good fit for what we do. The next thing we will change is adding some more literature, adding some more agile methods and throwing out some stuff that seems to be obvious anyway.

8.3 Management Career

When we changed our management structure and the people filling the corresponding roles, we realized that we needed to educate them as well. Our first step was to offer all managers participation in our Management 3.0 classes. About half of them jumped at the opportunity, the others didn't. Then we did a short training on labor law, which was quite helpful in understanding our legal obligations. Since project negotiations and sales tasks are important in these roles, we also hired external experts and conducted trainings for these topics. Around that time, we

8.3 Management Career

Table 8.3 Differences between the specialist and the consulting career

	JC	C	SC	MC	SMC
Business development & project sales	–	Rarely helps out	Occasional technical sales support	Distinct: uncovers technical opportunities and communicates these to the sales team; designs solution concepts; implements proof of concepts	Particularly strong: uncovers technical opportunities and communicates these to the sales team; designs solution concepts; implements proof of concepts; technical customer representative for proof of concepts
Responsibility	Own work	Own work	Technical subproject responsibility	Technical project responsibility	Technical topic ownership for customers on program level
Trainings	Contributes to training program development	Contributes to training program development and conducts training	Creates training programs and conducts trainings	Creates training programs and conducts trainings	Creates training programs and conducts trainings
Publications	–	Writes blog posts	Writes blog posts	Writes blog posts and professional articles	Writes blog posts and professional articles
Conferences	–	Visits conferences	Visits conferences	Delivers speeches on conferences	Delivers speeches on conferences
Assets and frameworks	–	Contributes to asset development	Contributes to asset development	Develops assets and is accountable for them	Accountable for multiple assets and/or frameworks

Table 8.4 Competency framework for Scrum Masters

	Adept	Practitioner	Expert	Lead
General expectations to meet	Accompany a more experienced colleague in engagements	Doing a good job alone in a single rollout or Scrum Master project with a single team	Doing a good job alone in a department-wide rollout of agile methods, leading up to three Scrum Teams as Scrum Master	Usually not working as Scrum Master. Instead leading organization-wide introductions of agile methods, doing organizational change, advising management
Agile Organizational Development	–	Adept	Practitioner	Expert
Appearance	Professional	Technically competent	Radiating reliability and trust up to middle management	Radiating reliability and trust up to top management
Trainings to have visited	Any Scrum training	Moderation/ facilitation skills training	Professional Scrum Master course, Professional Scrum Product Owner course, Professional coaching training, courses that correspond to her aptitude	Organizational change seminar, Management 3.0 workshop
Mentor	–	The mentor needs to be sure the mentee is perceived as practitioner by all customers	The mentor needs to be sure the mentee is perceived as expert by all customers	The mentor needs to be sure the mentee is perceived as lead by all customers
Coaching	–	The practitioner is being coached and delivers coaching in simple situations, following preparation by more experienced colleagues	Internal coaching of adepts and practitioners while being coached by an expert. The expert is able to deliver coaching without preparation even in difficult situations.	Is being coached by other leads, especially focusing on how to be a role model for the company and business unit values. The lead can coach even the most difficult situations spontaneously without a second thought.

(continued)

Table 8.4 (continued)

	Adept	Practitioner	Expert	Lead
Certificates	Professional Scrum Master I	Professional Scrum Master II	Professional Scrum Master III	Professional Scrum Product Owner II
Practical experience	Optional	A total experience of 1 year or more and at least 6 months of experience in a Scrum role; at least one project in the role of Scrum Master	At least 2 years of Scrum experience as Scrum Master	At least 5 years of Scrum experience and at least 3 years of Scrum Master experience
Customer projects	–	Having accompanied a more experienced Scrum Master in at least three different projects with three different teams, each lasting several weeks or more	Filling the Scrum Master role for at least two different Scrum Teams, totaling at least 2 years	Filling the Scrum Master role in at least five different projects. One of the projects must be small (one team) and one of them must be large (ten teams or more)
Reading requirements	Read a book about Scrum and the Scrum Guide (Schwaber & Sutherland, 2017)	Read the following books: Schwaber (2004) and Cohn (2009)	Read the following books: Derby and Larsen (2006), Kniberg (2012), Schwaber and Sutherland (2012), Schwaber (2007), Appelo (2016), Maximini (2015), Eckstein (2009) and Ries (2011)	Appelo (2010)
Providing training	–	Co-training short introductory workshops	Providing training alone	Providing training alone
Publications	–	Writing a first blog post or article alone	Writing blog posts or articles and leading forum discussions	Writing articles and potentially books
	–	–	Delivering talks	Delivering talks

(continued)

Table 8.4 (continued)

	Adept	Practitioner	Expert	Lead
Conference visits				
Community activities	–	Discussing agile topics with other practitioners, inside or outside the company	Active participation in the Scrum community outside NovaTec	Being known in the community, at least regionally
Management and leadership	–	–	Reading everything written by Tom DeMarco, Lohmann (2012) and Collins (2001)	Reading everything you get your hands on
Traditional project management	–	–	Successfully complete at least a university course on project management	Successfully complete at least a university course on project management
Other agile methods	–	Know some, e.g. Kanban, Lean Startup, or eXtreme Programming	Being adept for at least Kanban and eXtreme Programming	Being able to use other agile methods, tailor them, and teach them
K.O.-criteria	–	Command and control thinking; doesn't speak the language of the customer; doesn't volunteer for the role	Command and control thinking; doesn't speak the language of the customer; doesn't volunteer for the role; doesn't actively live by agile values	Command and control thinking; doesn't speak the language of the customer; doesn't volunteer for the role; doesn't actively live by agile
Team dynamics and life cycles	–	Read Riemann (1985) and Salzberger-Wittenberg (2002)	Research events and visit one training	Research events and visit one training

started to use monetary numbers for contribution margins and sales, so we had to learn how to deal with these as well. We did this internally.

As you can see, all mandatory training aspects concerned traditional management skills. They were focusing more on administration than on visionary leadership. Management 3.0 was the only exception, but even the relatively small nudge one gets in a 2-day course wasn't enjoyed by everybody.

From my point of view, the reason for this is that we still have not yet built a skill matrix for management. This makes it difficult for managers to agree on which skills are required at all and which ones to work on next. We still have a long way to go there. When we build such a matrix, we definitely should include topics like modern leadership, team building, personality assessments, and so on. Especially fluffy "soft" topics are in short supply in our management team. We also should strengthen management by building a community of practice. Learning from each other and hearing from each other's issues can help to improve our joint leadership performance. While we do have management meetings today, they are not dedicated to learning and certainly not facilitated in a way that promotes openness and learning through failure.

8.4 Learnings

We experience people wanting to not only to rise up the ranks, but also wanting to grow horizontally. Therefore, a traditional hierarchical career path was not enough and we introduced both specialist and consulting career paths. To make this work, we had to introduce transparent requirements for each career level of each career path. In our case, these requirements only differ in some specific points. Especially sales activities and the degree to which somebody is perceived as the extraordinarily competent face of NovaTec are diverging. It is very handy to use such a competency framework in our development dialogues, or when an employee is thinking about what step to take next in his development. The competency levels defined by us are very specific to the area of expertise the employees are working in, so it requires some cognitive effort to define a set of requirements for other competence areas.

While we are doing a great job with building competency frameworks in most business units, we did not do this for our management. This makes it difficult for our managers to agree on which skills are required at all and which ones to focus on next. So far, our education was driven by momentary needs. While we served these needs promptly, for example with trainings on labor law and negotiation, we did not integrate these into a broader context. This leaves us with blind spots, especially when looking at "soft" topics like team building or personality assessments. We are also lacking a community of practice for leadership so we can learn from each other and create a safe-to-fail environment for management experiments.

Changing Processes 9

We have taken a broad look at the organization so far. We always investigated the same topic, leadership, but we viewed it from different angles. In doing this, I already described some of the process changes in detail. While I hope you got some ideas for your own situation from this, I do believe you should know about some other process changes we also made. Some of the following topics were not mentioned at all so far, others were briefly grazed. All of them should be interesting nevertheless. Let's shine a light on them!

9.1 Who Gets to Decide What?

One of the biggest challenges we encounter is the question of who gets to decide what. Having intransparent rules on this leads to dissatisfaction of employees, conflicts between individuals, people overstepping invisible borders, hitting a "glass ceiling," or not living up to the expectations of their managers by not taking decisions they are allowed to take. Management 3.0 offers a neat practice for this issue: Delegation Boards (cf. Management3.0f).

A Delegation Board is basically a decision grid with eight columns and a possible infinite number of rows. The columns show the extent of delegation, the rows state the types of decisions that are being delegated (cf. Fig. 9.1).

The process to fill the board is quite straightforward. The first thing we did was to print out Delegation Poker cards (cf. Management3.0g). Then we put a brown paper onto the wall and created the seven-level-grid on it (cf. Table 9.1).

We discussed what each level means until we reached consensus. In the beginning, this was not easy, because we were not clear about the perspective from which the levels must be seen. Once we added the perspective (the one sharing his power), consensus followed quickly (cf. Table 9.2).

This might sound straightforward, but having tried this with many teams, it seems to be the major difficulty for everybody new to this practice. We defined the levels as described in Table 9.3 (cf. Appelo, 2014, p. 100, 2016, p. 66):

© The Author(s), under exclusive license to Springer Nature Switzerland AG 2022
D. Maximini, *Agile Leadership in Practice*, Future of Business and Finance, https://doi.org/10.1007/978-3-031-15022-7_9

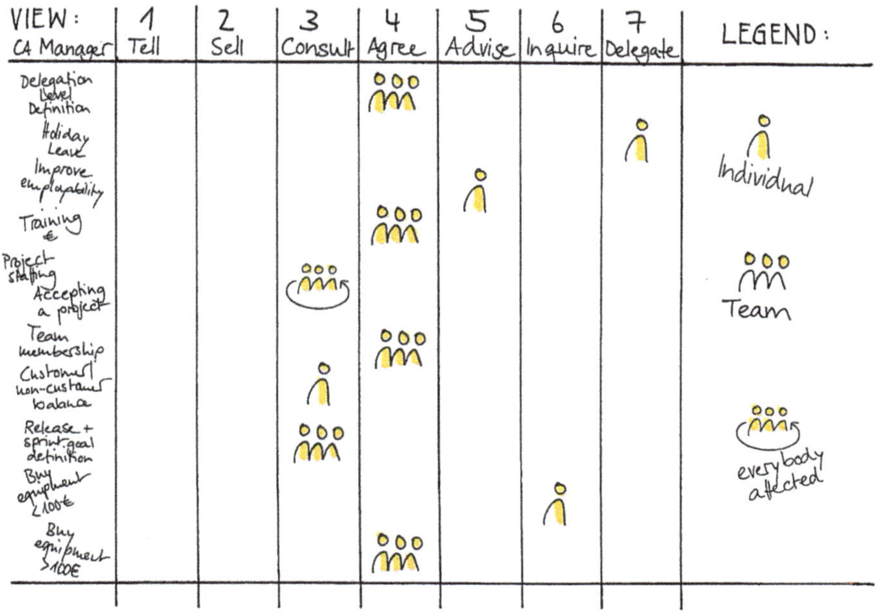

Fig. 9.1 Delegation Board

Table 9.1 Seven levels of delegation

	1- Tell	2- Sell	3- Consult	4- Agree	5- Advise	6- Inquire	7- Delegate

Table 9.2 Delegation levels viewed from the source of power

View: Manager	1- Tell	2- Sell	3- Consult	4- Agree	5- Advise	6- Inquire	7- Delegate

Once we understood all levels, a discussion on level four and higher embarked: Who exactly was the one being empowered? "The team" is such a vague term that it could mean anything and nothing. We reached the conclusion that, for our purposes, we needed three different groups who could be empowered:

9.1 Who Gets to Decide What?

Table 9.3 Delegation levels defined

#	Level	Definition
1	Tell	I tell the team what I decided and they have to go with it.
2	Sell	I make the decision, but I explain why I made it this way. Still, the team has to follow.
3	Consult	While I still make the decision, I will ask my team before I decide.
4	Agree	Both the team and I have to agree. So effectively, each has a right to veto, only consensus leads to a decision being made.
5	Advise	I will give my opinion to the team, but they decide and I have to follow.
6	Inquire	The team makes the decision, but I will ask about it and will be informed.
7	Delegate	I don't even need to know about the decision, the team handles such matters themselves.

- Each individual
- Everybody affected by the decision, as a team
- The full team

Whenever a group was empowered, we decided that the group could only exercise it with a "consent," meaning that every single person has the right to veto a decision, but not everybody has to agree. The difference to "consensus" is that in a consent situation it is okay to be neutral while in a consensus situation every single person has to actively agree. We then started figuring out what level of empowerment was appropriate for what kind of decision.

The Management 3.0 rules of Delegation Poker state that the manager has the final say on what delegation level to choose. This makes sense since the whole process wouldn't work if the one holding power was deprived of it, without any chance of having a say in it. At the end of the day, the manager will still be accountable to the outside world for what happens in her area of influence, no matter how much power she delegates or not. Still, I didn't like this rule, because we would start a new practice exercising old beliefs while trying to establish agile management thinking. Therefore, we started pokering the question: "Who has the final say about delegation levels?"

It took a while to get used to Delegation Poker, but finally we agreed on "Agree." Now both the team and I have a veto-right, and neither they nor I can decide on a specific level without the other party. This felt better and more democratic than just leaving the power with the manager. However, we still had to figure out who exactly would get the right to veto. The whole team? A subset of the team? Each individual?

We used three different corners in the room and started with multi-dimensional Delegation Poker: We not only had to show the card reflecting our opinion in numbers, we also had to walk to the corner signifying the group being empowered. This worked very well, and we soon had our first entry on the board (cf. Table 9.4). With each new entry on the board, I would have one vote and the team would have one vote.

Now that we were familiar with the practice, we first identified all types of decisions we thought we should discuss, which resulted in Table 9.5. We also

Table 9.4 Deciding on delegation levels

View: manager	1—Tell	2—Sell	3—Consult	4—Agree	5—Advise	6—Inquire	7—Delegate
Deciding on delegation levels				Team			

Table 9.5 Topics to decide about

View: manager	1—Tell	2—Sell	3—Consult	4—Agree	5—Advise	6—Inquire	7—Delegate
Deciding on delegation levels				Team			
Vacation leave approval							
What to do to increase employability							
Education budget use							
Project acceptance and staffing							
Team membership							
Project/slack balance							
Release and Sprint goals							
Buy equipment <100€							
Buy equipment >100€							

decided that whatever was not on the board would be left to common sense of the employee or fall automatically back to the manager. In other words, I encouraged the team to do the best they could, knowing that the decision officially resided with me and I could veto theirs, if needed.

During the Delegation Poker process, some interesting discussions took place. For example, I wanted to put the "What to do to increase employability" (so the decision which books to read, what trainings to choose, what to learn next, etc.) on "Delegate," because I believe everybody should do this alone, not necessarily with the manager. The team however initially wanted "Consult" because they wanted to incorporate my thinking. We finally agreed on "Advise," which leaves the responsibility with the team but allows them to consider my suggestions.

The final board had the following entries (cf. Table 9.6):

This board remained valid for about 2 years. We often discussed if we should change something, but only after the 2-year period did we actually do so. The trigger was the change in the corporate procedure for overtime compensation (cf. Sect. 6.3). We figured we should discuss how to handle this topic rather than leaving the decision with me. When working on the board, we quickly pokered everything on it again, which resulted in a couple of changes (cf. Table 9.7). For your convenience, the table shows the first version values in brackets if today's values deviate.

This board is our most recent one and we still use it in our day-to-day business. As you can see, there is a trend for items to move to the right. Nothing was moved left so far. The last item was added to the table. The complicated way it is phrased implies

9.1 Who Gets to Decide What?

Table 9.6 Delegation Board version one

View: manager	1—Tell	2—Sell	3—Consult	4—Agree	5—Advise	6—Inquire	7—Delegate
Deciding on delegation levels				Team			
Vacation leave approval							Individual
What to do to increase employability					Individual		
Education budget use				Team			
Project acceptance and staffing			Everybody affected				
Team membership				Team			
Project/slack balance			Individual				
Release and Sprint goals			Team				
Buy equipment <100€						Individual	
Buy equipment >100€				Team			

correctly that it was not an easy discussion. We hit a major conflict within the team: One part of the team emphasized that they should be able to compensate for their overtime, no matter how the company fared and no matter what the consequences of their actions were. Another fraction of the team took the opposing stance and stated that they always needed to put the interests of the organization first, because if the organization suffered, we would all suffer. One person even stated that he didn't need overtime compensation at all and we shouldn't discuss it. We were unable to agree on how to solve the issue. This led to the rather complicated entry on the board and the removal of another card, stating how to deal with several days of overtime compensation at once. Since we couldn't agree, it defaulted back to me, practically leaving it at level three (consult). We agreed to discuss it again when the need arose for somebody. Within the last year, this need did not arise. It will be interesting to see how this works out when we discuss it again after having had time to ponder it.

Whenever we show our Delegation Board to someone, especially people working for big companies, it results in three critical discussions: How can it work that vacation leave is a seven? How can you handle a four in team membership? How is it possible that you give budget power to the team?

The first two questions will be explained in more detail in Sects. 9.4 and 9.5. Let me share our view on delegating budget power to the team with you.

Table 9.7 Today's Delegation Board

View: manager	1—Tell	2—Sell	3—Consult	4—Agree	5—Advise	6—Inquire	7—Delegate
Deciding on delegation levels				Team			
Vacation leave approval							Individual
What to do to increase employability					(Individual)	Individual	
Education budget use				Team			
Project acceptance and staffing			(Everybody affected)	Everybody affected			
Team membership				Team			
Project/slack balance			(Individual)		Team		
Release goals			Team				
Sprint goals			(Team)	Team			
Buy equipment <100€						(Individual)	Individual
Buy equipment >100€				Team			
Take single-day leave for overtime, if holiday leave is planned for the rest of the year (max 3 days still open)						Individual	

Neither our team members want to ask for approval for every single thing they need nor do I want to have to validate every small item that needs to be purchased. My team consists of responsible adults who know their own and the team's profitability, so they are fully capable of making such decisions. They have all the information they need. We chose 100€ as a reasonable amount everybody can spend on a single purchase, but we probably could triple the amount and it would still work. Bigger purchases are on "Agree," because this forces the team to discuss the need among themselves first. This proved to be quite helpful, because more efficient and economical solutions were identified. One example: "I want to order a moderation suitcase."—"Why don't you take the team suitcase? We can reassign it to you."—"Oh, I didn't know we had one. . . ."

We have now used a Delegation Board for several years. I am not completely sure whether we will discover new categories to improve us further still, and if we do, we are always happy making improvements when it becomes obvious that they make sense. In fact, I believe the Delegation Board is far more powerful than the information printed on it. We have not experienced any negative effects so far. On the contrary, clarifying the decision types and agreeing on delegation levels helped us tremendously to grow as a team. It also helped to speed up decisions and to save time for me as a manager.

We also taught this practice to the other competence area managers and some of them rapidly adopted it. Others are still hesitant and are waiting for more experiences to become evident. We also discussed using such a board for describing the relationship between the management board and our competence area managers. While we all agreed that this would be wise, we haven't done it yet. The reason is due to the additional freedoms the competence area managers received in phases two and three. Today, they are allowed to hire their own people, to decide on salary, to design their own business unit processes, and much more. Living up to these new expectations drove our focus more than the need to clarify what other additional decisions we should be allowed to make. In time and with increased maturity, the scope of responsibility will very likely change again.

9.2 SMILE

You already read some information about SMILE in Sect. 5.3. Let's take a closer look at this very interesting topic, even though some of the information repeats again here.

SMILE is our employee-led improvement system. The word stands for the goal: We want to make employees smile by improving issues the employees care about. Every employee who wants to participate in this endeavor is welcome to join, there is no elitist selection process, and there is no manager on the SMILE committee. The idea was initiated by today's feel-good manager, and in the early days I joined the endeavor upon his request to help nurture the young and beautiful plan. After a short period, I realized that my participation was no longer necessary because the other people in this group had gained so much self-assurance and routine in the process

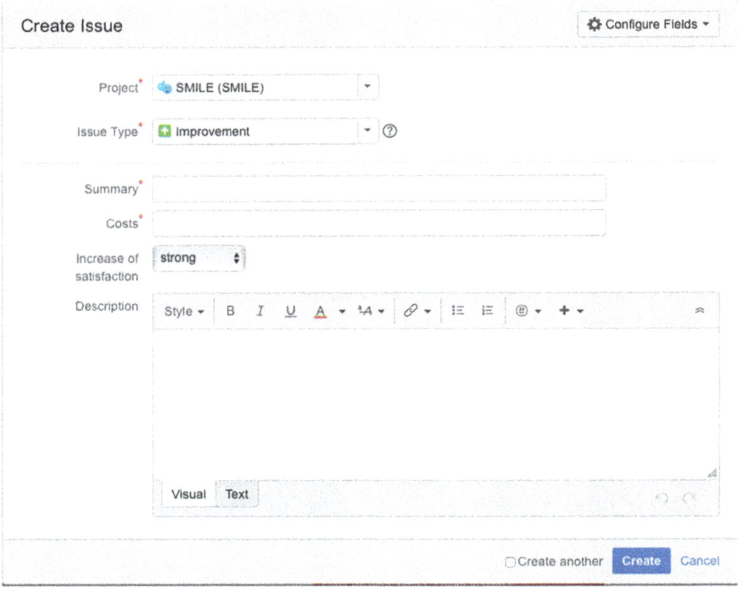

Fig. 9.2 SMILE idea entry form

that my future involvement might start inhibiting the whole idea. So, I withdrew and rejoice each quarter when I see what new cool ideas have been implemented.

In SMILE, any employee can suggest as many ideas as they want, by just entering a ticket into a simple ticketing system, set up for this purpose. They are supposed to enter the benefit and the costs of their idea, assisted by a member of the SMILE team (cf. Fig. 9.2).

Just having the idea in the system is not enough though. It must be ensured that the idea can actually be implemented if it is chosen. To clarify this, the person who put the idea into the system works with the experts for the topic (e.g., our central and technical services departments) and the SMILE team. If it cannot be done, it needs to be refined in a way that it becomes achievable. Once an idea is sufficiently spelled out, it can be voted on by all employees. To facilitate this, an email is sent out by the SMILE team, reminding everybody to cast their votes. Every employee can vote once for every single idea, no matter how many ideas are in the system. It is also possible to actively vote against ideas if somebody thinks we definitely should not implement it. We had to tweak the system to find a workaround for this feature, but it works for us now. Whoever is motivated enough to vote against an idea is also motivated enough to use the workaround. Results are calculated by summing up all the votes for the idea and subtracting all the votes against it.

Every quarter, the top-voted ideas are implemented by the SMILE team. Depending on the costs associated with the idea, a differing number of minimum votes is required (cf. Table 9.8).

9.2 SMILE

Table 9.8 SMILE vote minimums

Budget needed for implementation	Required minimum total votes
Up to 4999€	20
5000€ and beyond	30
10,000€ and beyond	40
15,000€ and beyond	50
Etc.	Etc.

That means if you want to buy additional equipment that costs 7000€, you will need 30 votes. Let's say in the first quarter you got 29 people voting for the idea and 10 people voting against it. This leaves you with a total of 19 votes, which means the idea won't be implemented this quarter. Any idea can stay in the system for 1 year. If it doesn't receive sufficient votes in that time period, it is declined. In the case of your additional equipment, you would still have three more quarters to rally support for your idea. Experience shows that this doesn't help though. Good ideas are voted for quickly, ideas that aren't chosen within two quarters won't ever come to life.

For implementing SMILE ideas, the management board provides a yearly budget of 50,000 Euro. Refer to Table 9.9 to learn which ideas have been implemented so far.

If an idea with sufficient votes is out of scope for SMILE, it is highlighted to the management board. Management then decides what to do, and either implements a change within the next quarter or explains to the employees why the situation will remain as is. This is highly appreciated by the employees and has a positive impact on happiness. It also means that management has an additional feedback cycle with the broader community. Table 9.10 shows a small sample of ideas highlighted by SMILE and implemented by our management team:

As one can expect, not everything is a walk in the park with this system. Sometimes people are unhappy because their idea wasn't voted for. In some cases, when the idea is outside the scope of SMILE, people are frustrated because management decided against their idea. We also encounter situations when someone wants their idea to see the light of day, but is unwilling to gather the necessary information for it. In the case of the snack dispenser, matters are even worse: Every item costs 1€. This is not much. The food can just be taken out of the dispenser and there is an honesty box for the employees to put their money in. We learned that some people just don't, leaving everybody else to pay for them. Since the box is set up in an area where customers have access, we don't know if it's our own people stealing or if it's our customers feeling entitled to free snacks, therefore we didn't remove the dispenser. However, this is just one example that didn't work so well—overall the experience is extraordinarily positive. We don't want to miss out having this system available to us!

Table 9.9 SMILE ideas and costs

Year	Idea	Costs
2015	Setting up a relaxation and first-aid room	377 EUR
2015	Providing special wireless mice for all consultants	5750 EUR
2015	Use different coffee beans in our coffee machines (trial)	129 EUR
2016	Use different coffee beans in our coffee machines (1-year budget)	5778 EUR
2016	Replace desks with height-adjustable ones (first batch)	8307 EUR
2016	Get ventilators for hot summer days	2529 EUR
2016	Establish a sofa corner in the canteen	4148 EUR
2016	Get better whiteboards for effective cleaning	1867 EUR
2016	More ventilators for hot summer days	1966 EUR
2016	Get a second soccer table	758 EUR
2016	Establish our own canteen system, allowing everybody to have lunch in the company (basic equipment)	600 EUR
2016	Exchange fridges for ones with freezing compartments to include space for ice cream	2150 EUR
2016	Buy more height-adjustable desks with the rest of our 2016 budget (second batch)	21,897 EUR
2017	Buy a small snack dispenser where employees can buy food	31 EUR
2017	Buy more height-adjustable desks with the rest of our 2016 budget (third batch)	8307 EUR
2017	Provide professional barbecue equipment so employees can have barbecue for lunch	2673 EUR
2017	Buy a professional coffee machine	9531 EUR
2017	Get new additional types of tea	244 EUR
2017	Purchase ventilators for meeting rooms for hot summer days	514 EUR
2017	Provide access to an online education platform	11,760 EUR
2017	Buy more height-adjustable desks with the rest of our 2017 budget (fourth batch)	16,940 EUR

9.3 Project Selection

Back in phase one, projects were solely assigned by management board members. That effectively meant that somebody who hardly knew you would send you to a project he deemed appropriate for you. In some cases, this even meant as far as Saudi Arabia—even though saying "no" was accepted there. This also meant that it took a lot of courage for a regular employee to voice concerns, because a board member

9.3 Project Selection

Table 9.10 SMILE ideas implemented by management

Allowing travel time to count as regular working time
Increase data volume in our mobile phone contracts
Dual-screen setups for desks with docking stations
Transmit important meetings virtually, so people working offsite can participate
Improving the way we log our working times
Replacing the projectors in meeting rooms with more modern equipment including video
...and many more

was just so much further up the command chain. In phase two, this started to change. On the one hand, management capacity was needed elsewhere. On the other hand, we had grown too big for board members to assign us all to individual projects. On top of that, our projects in the agile domain differed significantly from application development projects: We often only stay for months with customers, rarely for years, and hardly ever full-time for more than a couple of weeks. This required far more attention to reassigning people than was sensible and realizable with a top-down approach. For these reasons, the assignment process was changed for the whole company. Today, board members only suggest assignments, and they only do this for very large or strategic projects. The decisions are made by project leads for large projects (in combination with the affected competence area managers and in consultation with the responsible branch office managers) and competence area managers manage it for small projects. Of course, the consultants intended for the project participate in the decision and usually have a veto-right.

This also makes sense when considering people's changing preferences. Twenty years ago, people were far more eager to travel a lot and to quickly climb up the career ladder. Today, people seem to favor their private lives and career preferences look different (cf. Chap. 8). Throughout the company, including our agile team, project assignment is considered extremely important. If individual needs aren't met, this process becomes a major pain point.

We tackled this issue in our business unit in two steps. The first step was to agree on the delegation level (cf. Sect. 9.1). The second was to agree on a corresponding strategy (cf. Sect. 6.1).

Our Delegation Board discussion was very interesting. When we looked at project staffing, the team initially voted for "Advise," because they thought everybody should choose their favorite projects themselves. While I generally agreed, I didn't want to let go of the final say in case the company's survival was threatened. On top of that, I am formally accountable for our revenues. In the end, we agreed on "Consult." Approximately 2 years later we changed that to "Agree," because trust and ownership have risen considerably throughout the whole team. Actually, I would probably accept "Advise" as well and leave it to the team, but the team does not seem to want the full responsibility there, yet. Having project selection on "Agree" means it's not only okay to say "no" to a specific project, it's formally documented. This reinforces the fact that the employee, in agreeing to a project, is jointly responsible for their own satisfaction in the project role. In delegating this way ensures that all personal needs can be accommodated, whenever possible.

Our competence area strategy spells out some additional parameters we consider with every new project:

- We focus on customers who are 1 h or less away (yellow zone) and are no more than 250 km away from where we live (red zone).
- We can serve these customers while sleeping in hotels less than five times per month.
- These rules are not valid if there are no alternatives, strategic goals counter them, or we as a team want the project for other reasons.

These rules allow us to make sound decisions and to set the corresponding expectations with our team. People are happy with their projects and the way they are involved in the decision-making. This is important for our customers too, because happy consultants do a better job for them.

The problem with this strong employee focus is that sometimes nobody volunteers for important customer projects. We encountered several situations in which we had good business reasons to jump on a project that was outside the comfort zone of the available people in the team (even though still within our strategic boundaries), but they had personal reasons to shy away from it. Since we set the delegation level to "Agree," I cannot just force somebody to take on a specific project. I have to explain, ask, bid, or beg. This is not working well, because it triggers my emotional abyss and thus creates conflict. It also means that we cannot satisfy the whole available market as easily or quickly as other companies, which might pose a problem when times get tougher. Also, people get spoiled. The more cherry-picking people in the team do, the more cherry-picking is desired by everybody. This makes it even more difficult to bite the bullet when necessary for any specific individual situation.

We are trying to get out of this vicious circle by changing the team system. We will soon establish a new role, filled by a new hire, who will then help people to get out of their comfort zones. While I personally am not able to stay rational on this topic, this person will be. If this doesn't solve the issue, we will continue looking for other ways to tweak the system, satisfy the market quickly, and keep everybody happy with their projects.

9.4 Holiday Leave

Signing off holiday leave sheets is standard business for many managers around the globe. I never thought this made sense, as when I work with highly-paid employees who hold university degrees and manage multi-million Euro projects, I should expect them to be capable of managing their own absence. In addition, our business model puts our customers in the driver seat, making them our top priority when discussing leave. Once the customer is happy, chances are minimal that there could be other reasons to prevent people from flying off to their favorite beach resort. We obviously have some areas, such as our internal IT staff, who need to keep up an agreed service level every day. They are able to manage that themselves as well. When I assumed the position of competence area manager all I did with our leave applications was to blindly sign them off, because when putting it into the system, the employee only could send it to me when they ticked a box verifying that they discussed their leave with their customers. My fellow competence area managers did it pretty much the same way. Therefore, we changed the process throughout the company, putting holiday leave applications on auto-approve. This happened at the same time as allowing people to be compensated for more than 4 days of overtime a year.

This step was not as simple as it seems. For example, some managers feared that due to the coupling of these two changes employees might collectively stay home for several weeks during Christmas, stripping our customers bare of support. This didn't happen. Others thought this would deprive managers of their control over their employees. Let me tell you, we actually never had this kind of control in the first place since our employees are neither slaves nor stupid. Our people take their responsibility seriously and act accordingly. In the end, our IT system was the bottleneck. Once it was reprogrammed, it worked like a charm and I definitely don't want to miss this relief of useless administrative overhead.

9.5 Hiring New Employees

In phase one our hiring process was inacceptable. We had (and in some areas still have) really boring job advertisements, not reflecting our true selves, our vision or our values. Well, we had not specified these back then, but that's a different story. Almost all new hires were found through personal networks, not via our job ads. When we invited a candidate, this person had to talk to a member of the management board, usually supported by somebody from the competence area that person would most likely join. The job interview was conducted in a very traditional way: asking questions, getting answers. Then, the member of the board decided to hire or reject the candidate. There was no onboarding process, so when somebody joined the company, it depended very much on the thoughtfulness (and overload) of the responsible competence area manager how welcome the new person felt.

Since phase three, this is changing considerably. Throughout the organization, the competence area managers conduct the interviews and make the hiring decisions now. Board members are only involved for contract questions or if the applicant has special requirements. Also, we are working on a global hiring strategy. Our business unit jumped ahead and already implemented a largely improved process.

For the beginning of the process, we created a new job advertisement that focuses on emotions rather than a checklist of facts (cf. Fig. 9.3).

We removed stock photos and put real pictures of our team onto the page instead. Our vision and mission are central to the advertisement. Usually the job description and required skills cover the lion's share of job ads. We shortened that down to a

Fig. 9.3 2017 agile job advertisement

simple message: "You know what an agile coach does, otherwise you wouldn't be interested in this job. Therefore, we won't bore you with lengthy descriptions. Tell us who you are!"

Alongside this message, applicants get an email address and a picture of me, so they see who will deal with their request. They also know that it's not some central HR person but rather the person they will report to if their application is accepted. Building up this page took one of our team members less than half a day. Once it was up, we received a first application within 2 days, which was really special for us, not having received any application through our job ads before.

If we invite an applicant, we handle both the interview and the hiring decision as "Agree" (delegation level four). That means, both the team and I have one vote and can say "no." As we need two "yes" votes to proceed, any "no" rejects the applicant. Whenever anybody wants to join our team, no matter if he is an internal or an external candidate, we conduct a two-step process. Mostly, both steps happen on the same day. Firstly, I screen the candidate (sometimes this is the second step and the team gets the first call). Since I do have veto power, I can exercise it right away. This keeps the dismal candidates away from the team. The ones that are acceptable or even good are passed along to the team. This means we go to the team room and start a friendly discussion with the candidate. If we sense the need for a deeper dive, we challenge the candidate with tougher questions. Usually, we end this with a joint lunch, provide the candidate with clear feedback, and sleep it over before we vote on the candidate the next day. This process is very transparent and appreciated by everyone involved. Even candidates who were eventually turned down thanked us for our openness.

The process does take about half a day with as many people from the team as possible. However, if we don't invest in our people, then what else is worth investing in? This experience brings the team even closer together and creates a very strong bond of trust both within the old team and with the new members. So far, we have accepted about 25% of all applicants.

Once somebody is hired, he profits from an organization-wide onboarding process implemented by our feel-good manager. All new hires are welcomed on their first day, receive their equipment (computers, mobile phones, business cards, etc.), get general information, for example about HR topics, and get to know each other. The day before, their desks are prepared with little welcome presents. Then, they are sent on a scavenger hunt that requires them to rush through the whole company and helps them to recognize buildings, departments, and people—both physically and digitally. The whole onboarding process takes one and a half days, leaving the new hires highly motivated and well informed for their new jobs.

We are still improving all stages of this process, but we probably already achieved 80% of the possible value. The next step is to adapt this approach for all business units.

9.6 Career Coaching

The introduction of career coaching is one of the most important changes we made so far. It is also the most powerful alteration to our operational structure. Employee growth is a primary measure to get our organization ahead, and career coaching plays toward this goal. Viewed from the outside, the purpose of this role is quite simple: Conduct development dialogues with employees, as a delegate of the accountable competence area manager. Examining it a little bit closer, a whole new leadership approach reveals itself. The first new aspect is that the disciplinary leader no longer directly exerts her influence over her employees' development. Effectively, this means a loss of power for her. The second aspect is how the service of development dialogues is delivered. In top-down organizations it very often happens that the boss tells the worker what steps to do next. If the worker is lucky, his boss asks him about his wishes first, and then decides. This is not how career coaching works. A career coach makes use of the two stances "coaching" and "mentoring" as well as the corresponding techniques. In the coaching stance, the career coach disassociates herself from the content the coachee is talking about. She is not there to judge or to advise, her job is to help the coachee uncover new insights. This is done by actively listening to what the coachee says and asking powerful questions, digging deeper and deeper, all the way to the underlying motivators. Once found, the coach helps the coachee to define steps to improve the situation. This again is done by applying questioning techniques, not by giving advice.

In the mentoring stance, things are slightly different. The career coach will use coaching techniques as well, but when it comes to the point where the coachee needs to define actions, the career coach will offer some experience or ideas. Choosing them or doing something completely different is then up to the coachee again.

Consulting, meaning providing solutions for the coachee, is not part of the career coach's job.

Everything a career coach does is focused on individual professional development. Sometimes, this touches personal development as well, but only as long as this is needed to get the professional skills of the coachee to the next level. A career coach is neither a psychotherapist nor a life coach. She is a highly effective professional coach and mentor for her coachees.

The process used for this throughout NovaTec is fairly simple. First, people who are interested in the role get trained in the art of coaching. It's a 6-day training, focused very much on learning specific career coaching techniques and practicing them in a safe environment. After this training, they start to coach one or two coachees as often as they want, but at least once a quarter. Coachees can choose or ditch their coaches as they please, therefore the coaches need to make an effort and focus very much on their coachees. Once a month, all career coaches meet and exchange their experiences, sharing good practices, what worked and what failed. They also advise each other and define coaching guidelines that are used throughout the company. As you can see, we are investing heavily in this aspect of our leadership culture. We believe coaching is an essential service for our employees in times of change.

It's a general rule that the topics of career coaching sessions are chosen by the coachee while the methods are chosen by the coach. This means the responsibility for individual development resides with the coachee, not with the coach or the manager. If the coachee chooses to talk about a specific project situation, honing a certain skill, advancing in rank or how to earn more money, this is what the development dialogue will be about. It's a good idea to first discuss this with the career coach and only approach the competence area manager once the career coach is engaged. As soon as a development dialogue between a career coach and an employee produces the need for training or other means that involve costs, the need is highlighted to the competence area manager or, depending on the business unit, to the team. The career coaches formally have no right to decide anything, unless explicitly granted by the competence area manager. Their skills are their power. They can help their coachees to see new opportunities and to learn more about themselves. The good thing about this is that they never have a hidden agenda, which is sometimes the case with managers. The coaches are able to fully focus on their coachees and fully assume their perspective.

Essentially, we use a multitude of professional coaches to get our employees ahead. We also expect our managers to learn at least the coaching basics and use these in their daily work. Focusing on development and growth rather than law and order makes a huge difference in our working atmosphere.

Not everything works perfectly though. Some people were pushed into the role of career coach, which doesn't work at all. Some others volunteered for the role but don't show any talent for it. Both groups will have to step out of the role again soon. In some instances, employees shower their coaches with all their private problems, trying to avoid therapy costs. Some freshly baked coaches didn't notice this in the beginning, running into a dead end with their coachees. This will hopefully solve itself with growing experience. The most dangerous mistake we tried to make was to infuse the career coach role with disciplinary power though. The reasoning behind it was that our management board thought about how to scale business units, effectively delegating tasks of the competence area managers. Unfortunately, allowing career coaches to hold power over their coachees poisons their relationship in a way that makes it impossible for the coaches to fulfill their career coaching duties. Coachees tend to hold back when they fear—even unconsciously—their coach might reprimand them when the next promotion is due. Therefore, true coaching from a position of power is difficult at best, if not impossible. We were lucky to realize this before we allowed the idea to propagate and asked our management board to find another solution instead.

9.7 Organizing Management Work

Another process we changed was the way management organized their work. Back in phase one, there was no organization at all governing this. Every manager did what he thought was best for the company. There were board meetings of course, and the competence area managers talked to each other as well, but nobody aligned what they were doing. In phase two, both groups started to share their ideas and align their actions and starting from phase three, we organized our work with Kanban. This is fairly simple: We have a digital board that includes everything we want to discuss, decide, or do. In the beginning, work piled up quickly, so we introduced work-in-progress limits. As a management team, we cannot discuss more than five items at the same time, we cannot work on more than five items at once, and we cannot consider more than ten items to work on next. Every 2 weeks, we review the board and close as many tasks as possible. Individual managers look at the board more often of course.

Within our competence area of agile methods, we use Scrum. I fill the role of Product Owner, so it is my job to make sure we are working on the right things. I have to maximize the value we create by setting the right goals and creating the right vision. Our products are the employability of our team members, our performance in customer projects, our joint contribution margin, and the advancement of NovaTec toward an even more agile company. Everybody working in our business unit is part of the Development Team. The Scrum Master role rotates depending on the situation. We actually started to spin a bottle to define who will do it next. Our Sprint length is usually 4 weeks, allowing us to effectively collaborate on 4 days, because we all work in customer projects 4 days a week and only meet on Fridays. For our competence area, this works very well. This is no wonder, keeping in mind that we are all expert agile coaches, loving what we do.

We realized something important about self-organization though: It is not a done deal. Some people and tasks will never reach a high level of self-organization. This is true for everybody, even for agile coaches. In our case, sales tasks are pretty much neglected even by some of the senior employees. It seems that no process, not even an agile one, prevents us from inconsistent behaviors and thereby making bad decisions.

9.8 Learnings

Changing processes is absolutely necessary when moving toward a more agile way of working. Which ones you need to change is very dependent on your specific situation and the maturity level you have already reached. It is also important to consider employee satisfaction, therefore we tried to align our process changes with employee needs. We have been working on it for 7 years now—with varying degrees of focus and success—and we don't feel like being done anytime soon. It feels like the journey is the reward. No matter how much we change and how far we go: as soon as we reached the peak of a mountain, we discover that there are even higher and more beautiful mountains beyond it. In addition, the world around us keeps changing. Courage, determination, and allowing failure in order to learn from it are the key ingredients that help us keep hiking and climbing. Changing our leadership system toward agile does not have a clearly defined end-state. It is a journey that enables and requires us to keep improving all the time.

The Phases

This really short chapter is intended for you to look up the phases whenever you encounter them throughout this book. This will help you to keep the context in your mind so it is easier for you to understand certain situations and actions we took. If you want to get a more thorough description of the phases, please refer back to Sect. 1.6.

Phase one: My first years at NovaTec. I was a regular consultant and my impact at NovaTec was restricted to the team I was part of. Even there it was small. We were three people back then: Me, my boss, and my boss's boss.

At corporate level, the management board was trying to work together while first conflicts surfaced. Decision-making was centralized and stayed with the board, competence area managers were just responsible for content and held no power.

Phase two: A period of about 3 years, signified by a struggle inside the management board. Not much was decided on corporate level then, the competence areas were largely unmanaged by the board and all improvements were significantly inhibited. Changing anything was like walking through thick mud. Some business units were working quite well nevertheless, especially in terms of content production and education. The phase ended with the CEO leaving the company and two other managers entering the board.

Phase three: We were there in 2017, referenced as "today" throughout this book. In this phase, we were trying experiments on a large scale, affecting the whole company. This is where the big wheels were turned and an agile company was being created.

Appendix

This appendix provides you with some additional details. The following tables highlight numbers whereas the chapters above show graphics to make the information easier to digest. First, take a look at the Business area results of our agile methods (Table A.1).

You can also examine the corporate numbers more closely (Table A.2).

Table A.1 Business area results "agile methods"

	2014	2015	2016	2017
Sales	614,254€	829,865€	1,065,825€	1,507,457€
CM2	−280,425€	−82,587€	108,569€	335,828€
Net operating margin	n.a.	n.a.	10.2%	22.3%

© The Author(s), under exclusive license to Springer Nature Switzerland AG 2022
D. Maximini, *Agile Leadership in Practice*, Future of Business and Finance,
https://doi.org/10.1007/978-3-031-15022-7

Table A.2 NovaTec results

	2010	2011	2012	2013	2014	2015	2016	2017
Number of employees	101	121	139	159	164	153	166	193
Labor turnover rate (%)	7	12	14	4	9	16	13	10
Result per employee (%)	100	2	206	86	547	941	1610	3111
Result year over year (%)		−98	9234	−58	537	72	71	93
Average customer days per week ("C-Prod")	4.14	3.92	3.86	3.84	3.85	3.93	3.85	3.59

Abbreviations

C	Consultant
CA	Competence area, a business unit inside NovaTec
CAM	Competence area manager
CM1	Contribution Margin 1 (revenue minus direct costs)
CM2	Contribution Margin 2 (CM2 minus indirect costs)
C-Prod	Customer Productivity, the average number of days per week spent working for customers
ERP	Enterprise Resource Planning
HR	Human resources, or human relations
IT	Information Technology
JC	Junior Consultant
KPI	Key Performance Indicator
MBA	Master of Business Administration
MC	Managing Consultant
NPS	Net Promoter Score
SC	Senior Consultant
SMC	Senior Managing Consultant
SMILE	No acronym, it's our employee-led improvement system

Literature

Allen, T. (1984). *Managing the flow of technology*. MIT Press. ISBN: 9780262510271.
Appelo, J. (2010). *Management 3.0: Leading agile developers, developing agile leaders*. Addison-Wesley.
Appelo, J. (2014). *#Workout: Games, tools & practices to engage people, improve work, and delight clients*. Happy Melly Express. No longer available (replaced by Appelo 2016).
Appelo, J. (2016). *Managing for happiness: Games, tools, and practices to motivate any team*. Wiley.
Cohn, M. (2009). *Succeeding with agile. Software development using Scrum*. Addison-Wesley.
Collins, J. (2001). *Good to great: Why some companies make the leap...and others don't*. Harper Business.
Derby, E., & Larsen, D. (2006). *Agile retrospectives: Making good teams great*. Pragmatic Bookshelf.
Eckstein, J. (2009). *Agile Softwareentwicklung mit verteilten Teams*. dpunkt Verlag.
Gilb, T. (2005). *Competitive engineering: A handbook for systems engineering, requirements engineering, and software engineering using planguage*. Butterworth-Heinemann.
Kniberg, H. (2012). *Lean from the trenches: Managing large-scale projects with Kanban*. O'Reilly.
Lohmann, D. (2012). *Und mittags geh ich heim: Die völlig andere Art, ein Unternehmen zum Erfolg zu führen*. Linde Verlag.
Management3.0a. *Management 3.0 practices:Feedback wraps*. Management30.com. Accessed September 10, 2017, from https://management30.com/practice/feedback-wraps/
Management3.0b. *Management 3.0 practice:Moving motivators*. Management30.com. Accessed September 10, 2017, from https://management30.com/practice/moving-motivators/
Management3.0c. *Management 3.0 practices: Salaryformula*. Management30.com. Accessed September 16, 2017, from https://management30.com/product/workouts/salary-formula-compensation-plan/
Management3.0d. *Management 3.0 practices:Identity symbols*. Management30.com. Accessed September 17, 2017, from https://management30.com/product/workouts/workout-why-identity-symbols-matter-to-your-success/
Management3.0e. *Management 3.0 practices:Kudo box*. Management30.com. Accessed September 17, 2017, from https://management30.com/practice/kudo-box/
Management3.0f. *Management 3.0 practice: Delegation board*. Management30.com. Accessed December 30, 2017, from https://management30.com/practice/delegation-board/
Management3.0g. *Management 3.0 product:Delegation poker*. Management30.com. Accessed December 30, 2017, from https://management30.com/product/delegation-poker/
Management3.0h. *Teamcompetency matrix*. Management30.com. Accessed December 30, 2017, from https://management30.com/practice/competency-matrix/
Maximini, D. (2015). *The Scrum culture: Introducing agile methods in organizations*. Springer.
Pink, D. H. (2011). *Drive: The surprising truth about what motivates us*. Riverhead Books.

Ries, E. (2011). *The lean startup*. Crown Business.
Riemann, F. (1985). *Grundformen der Angst* (12th ed.). E. Reinhardt.
Salzberger-Wittenberg, I. (2002). *Psychoanalytisches Verstehen von Beziehungen: Ein Kleinianischer Ansatz*. Facultas.
Schein, E. H. (2009). *The corporate culture survival guide* (New and revised ed.). Jossey-Bass.
Schneider, W. E. (1999). *The reengineering alternative. A plan for making your current culture work* (Special reprint ed.). McGraw Hill.
Schwaber, K. (2004). *Agile project management with Scrum*. Microsoft Press.
Schwaber, K. (2007). *The enterprise and Scrum*. Microsoft Press.
Schwaber, K., & Beedle, M. (2002). *Agile software development withScrum* (Pearson International ed.). Prentice Hall.
Schwaber, K., & Sutherland, J. (2012). *Software in 30 days*. Wiley.
Schwaber, K., & Sutherland, J. (2017). *TheScrumguide*. Scrumguides.org. Accessed December 29, 2017, from http://scrumguides.org/docs/scrumguide/v2017/2017-Scrum-Guide-US.pdf
Sobel Lojesi, K., & Reilly, R. (2008). *Uniting the virtual workforce: Transforming leadership and innovation in the globally integrated enterprise*. Wiley. ISBN: 0470193956.
Stacey, R. D. (1996). *Strategic management & organisational dynamics: The challenge of complexity* (2nd ed.). Financial Times Management Publishing.
Statista. (2017a). *Arbeitslosenquote in Deutschland im Jahresdurchschnitt von 1995 bis 2017*. Statista. Accessed September 8, 2017, from https://de.statista.com/statistik/daten/studie/1224/umfrage/arbeitslosenquote-in-deutschland-seit-1995/
Statista. (2017b). *Monatliche Arbeitslosenquote in Baden-Württemberg von August 2016 bis August 2017*. Statista. Accessed September 8, 2017, from https://de.statista.com/statistik/daten/studie/155318/umfrage/arbeitslosenquote-in-baden-wuerttemberg/

Index

A
Authority, 2, 16, 17, 42, 43

B
Bonusly, 31, 32, 36, 86, 91

C
Career
    coaching, 73, 86, 87, 91, 121–123
    levels, 21, 25, 76–78, 89, 92, 94–96, 105
    models, 95, 96
    paths, 86, 95–105
Central functions, 4, 42
Chief fun officer
    CFO, 12, 35, 86, 91
Commitment, 33, 34, 39, 86
Competency frameworks, 102, 105
Competency matrix, 100
    See also Competency frameworks
Complexity, 48, 58, 97
Conflicts, ix, 13, 14, 16, 19, 20, 25, 35, 37, 47, 48, 58, 59, 93, 94, 98, 107, 111, 118, 125
Contribution margin, 4, 64–66, 69, 72, 74, 79–81, 84, 86, 104, 123, 129
Culture books, 28, 35

D
Delegation board, 49, 61, 107, 108, 111–113, 117
Delegation poker, 107, 109, 110

Department head, 21, 39, 41, 45, 50, 54, 61, 79
Development dialogues, 17, 18, 54–57, 85, 87, 100, 105, 121, 122

E
Employee turnover, 81, 82
Escalation, 23, 95
Experiment, vi, xi, 4, 6, 7, 9, 11, 13, 17, 25, 27, 29, 31, 83, 105, 125

F
Feedback, 5, 16, 21–23, 25, 26, 33, 34, 39, 50, 59, 67, 68, 74, 78, 79, 83, 96, 115, 120
Feedback Wraps, 14–16, 35
Feel-good manager, 68, 69, 89, 113, 121
Firing, 4, 32–34, 36, 93
Focus, ix, 4, 10, 12, 27, 28, 35, 38, 47, 54, 56, 57, 63–69, 71–73, 75, 78, 80–85, 99, 105, 113, 118, 122, 124

H
Happiness, v, 2, 27, 42, 44, 51, 63, 66–69, 71, 75–79, 81, 83, 84, 89, 115
Hierarchy, 10, 37, 38, 42, 50, 51, 90, 92
Hiring, 4, 32–34, 36, 88, 119–121
Holiday leave, 112, 118, 119

I
Identity symbol, 28, 29, 35
Information systems, 64, 66, 69, 71, 84

K
Kudo box, 29
Kudo Cards, 29–32, 35, 36, 85, 86, 91
Kudo Wall, 30, 31

M
Maturity, 25, 32, 33, 35, 59, 60, 113, 124
Money, 4, 17, 23–25, 31, 34, 35, 38, 39, 41, 45, 49–51, 54, 55, 57, 63–65, 71, 79–85, 87–90, 92, 93, 115, 122
Moving Motivators, 17, 18, 35, 85, 93

N
Net promoter score, 67, 75, 76, 84, 129

O
Organizational structure, ix, 1, 37–52, 79
Overtime, 83, 92, 110–112, 119

P
Performance appraisal, 13, 21–24, 35, 39, 55, 56
Personal maps, 11, 12, 35
Persons of trust, 23
Pizza budget, 55
  See also Pizza money
Pizza money, 88
Praise, 23, 29, 55, 78, 86, 91
Project selection, 116–118
Promotions, 18, 22, 78, 85, 86, 91, 93, 96, 97, 123

R
Respect, 10, 11, 60, 88
Rewards, ix, 1, 31, 32, 55, 85–94, 124
Risk, 21, 43, 51, 64, 67, 68, 83, 93

Role model, 13, 35, 61, 98, 99, 102

S
Salary
  distribution, 24, 25
  formula, 24, 27, 35, 93, 94
  negotiations, 19, 20, 24, 25
  systems, 20, 93, 94
  workshops, 20, 21, 25–27, 35
Scrum, 1, 4, 5, 9, 19, 29, 33, 37, 38, 63, 72–74, 100, 102–104, 123
Servant leadership, 59, 75, 98
SMILE, 67–69, 79, 86, 89–91, 113–117, 129
Structure, ix, 4, 21, 35, 38, 39, 41, 43, 44, 50, 51, 53, 92, 100, 121

T
Team, v, vii, ix, xiii, 3–6, 9–39, 41, 44–62, 65–68, 72–74, 81, 85–88, 91, 92, 95, 97, 99, 101–105, 107–115, 117–123, 125
360-degree-feedback, 21
Transparency, vii, 13, 18–27, 29, 35, 59, 62, 66, 78
Trust, 5, 9, 10, 13–19, 21, 23, 35, 37, 38, 44, 48, 51, 59, 62, 68, 74, 89, 102, 117, 121

V
Vacation, v, 33, 34, 110–112
  See also Holiday leave
Values
  core, 27, 28, 30
  stories, 28, 35
  wish, 27, 28, 30
Virtual distance, 46, 47, 49–51
Virtual teams, 48
Virtual working, 37, 46–52
Vision, x, 1, 28, 29, 45, 48, 51, 53, 54, 59, 63, 64, 67, 69, 71, 72, 74, 119, 123